# Andragogical Interventions

Krishna Nath Pandey, Ph. D

&

Satish Chandra

Published by Zorba Books, March 2023

Website: www.zorbabooks.com
Email: info@zorbabooks.com
Title: Andragogical Interventions
Author Name: Krishna Nath Pandey, Ph D & Satish Chandra


Printbook ISBN: 978-93-95217-52-1
Ebook ISBN: 978-93-95217-48-4



**Zorba Books Pvt. Ltd. (opc)**
Sushant Arcade,
Next to Courtyard Marriot,
Sushant Lok 1, Gurgaon – 122009, India

Printed by Manipal Technologies Limited
A1 & A2 Shivalli Industrial Area Manipal Udupi, Karnataka - 576104

Dedicated to Mr. Ram Naresh Singh, Chairman;
Damodar Valley Corporation for personifying friendship
through the thick and thin of our lives.

# CONTENTS

# LIST OF TABLES

# LIST OF FIGURES

# ACKNOWLEDGEMENT

There is no beginning and end either in life or in a book. This is largely due to the fact that the life is a unit of 'stream of consciousness 'and the book is an intermittent document which 'borrows' from those authors and researchers who have already contributed to a particular realm of the existing literature and every document drops the knowledge nuggets for future authors and researchers. However, we want to record the immense patience of our spouses, off springs and siblings.

Authors are thankful to Dr. Jitendra Yadav, Chancellor, SunRise University and Registrar Dr. Pankaj Gupta for allowing the use of all resources of that varsity. We are especially; thankful to Mr. K. Sreekant, CMD of POWERGRID, Dr. Vinod Kumar Singh, Director (HR) and Mr. R.K. Tyagi, Director (Asset Management) of POWERGRID for their guidance and support and additionally for making the authors 'cosy and comfortable' during the penning of this book.

Last, but not the least, authors acknowledge the time stolen from Ananya Ganesh for writing this book.

# PREFACE

There are three methods of teaching and learning, namely; pedagogy, andragogy and autonoetic method. The facilitators of learning in the institutionalised milieu quite often use these terms interchangeably. However pedagogy is largely used for teacher-taught method and ends with the secondary level. The tertiary level of education needs andragogy viz. learning by adults whereas autonoetic is a technique of 'lifelong learning'.

Since this scenario has been prevailing, therefore; the authors thought to contribute to the field of lifetime education for one and all alike.

The authors have tried their level best to provide a model catering to the needs of facilitators of learning, they do not claim to be authentic but pragmatic and prudent. It is hoped that this festschrift will serve as a catalyst to exhort the readers to look at learning as an odyssey in happiness.

The zenith of inquisitiveness and the pinnacle of self-motivation are the two legs which maybe needed to get ' more out of less' apropos the reading and perusal of this book besides browsing it wherever it is needed.

**– Authors**

# Chapter 1

# INTRODUCTION

"Quality Education," the fourth goal among the seventeen Sustainable Development Goals (SDGs) outlined by the United Nations, is "to ensure inclusive and equitable quality education and promote lifelong learning opportunities for all" (Peterson, 2009). It can be considered one of the most important SDGs for any country, as it is interlinked to several other SDGs, thus helping to achieve them as well. It is well known that education is critical in empowering liberation from the cycle of poverty, thus reducing inequalities while concurrently achieving gender equality, fostering tolerance between people, and contributing to more peaceful societies, and generating healthy life styles with an awareness of health and hygiene. The systematic knowledge attained through education has assumed the most determining role in the primary determinants of economic and social development and it shapes our life and our future (Ozturk, 2001).

In order to impart the quality education, the countries should have appropriate education ecosystem and an adequate policy framework. Over time, the education systems have evolved from knowledge imparted to pupils by a teacher through lectures in class using black boards as tools, to white boards, to overhead projectors, and finally to PowerPoint presentations and videos, and evaluating the learning outcomes of students through assignments and examinations. While the major evolution was in the form of the delivery mode of lectures or the way in which examinations are conducted, the traditional set up of in-class lectures to impart knowledge and evaluate learning outcomes of students through examinations and the submission of assignments has remained the same for most countries. Educators are the epitome in imparting education, thus making educators' skills and approaches the important factor of quality education: "Teachers can incorporate the competencies into their course and delivery to improve their effectiveness in the classroom, elevate their student knowledge, and make them better prepared and equipped for the business world" (Kanupriya M Bakhru, 2013).

There is no doubt that digital pedagogy in various forms will be the future of education, requiring adjustments in teaching and learning methodologies. The World Economic Forum notes that "65 percent of the children entering primary school in 2017 will have jobs that do not yet exist for which their education will fail to prepare them." In the case of India, according to a 2018 Report published by the Center for Monitoring Indian Economy (CMIE), "[t]here are around 31 million unemployed Indians seeking jobs" (TOI-Online, 2018). The job-seeking Indian youth can easily blame "lack of opportunity" as a reason for unemployment, but if this matter is perceived in its entirety, the reasons really are the lack of required technical as well as soft skills, such as writing, and listening and communicating effectively, which match the job profile adequately. The education system in India still depends and places emphasis on traditional system of teaching using lectures mainly based on textbooks, with hardly any change in the learning outcomes or profiles of the graduates. The Indian government does realize this, as professed in India's Draft National Education Policy 2019: "Instead of solely mechanistic rote learning, colleges and universities must encourage active learners to develop the abilities of independent, logical, and scientific thinking, creativity and problem solving, and decision-making. It must engage young people in national issues and concerns of the day" (Ministry of Human Resource Development 2019). The challenge now is for the education system to adapt itself accordingly in order to produce graduates who are acceptable by industry and enterprises. Furthermore, the pedagogy needs to be altered so that it not only provides knowledge, but also aims to inculcate an attitude in students that empowers them to acquire the knowledge and experience they will need throughout their lives, i.e. become life-long learners.

## 1.1 Statement of the Problem

With the advent of digital technology and the amount of boundless information and resources available on the Internet at a click of a button, knowledge of any topic/field is easily accessible. However, in order to apply it and to source pertinent/relevant information competently, both teachers and students need to be adequately educated. Various modern approaches have evolved to induce the "so- called 21st century skills such as critical thinking, communication, collaboration, creativity, information, media and technology skills" (James Bellanca and Ron Brandt, 2010); and for this, students need to be more active learners rather than just passive listeners in class, where the flow of information and knowledge is one way from instructor to students, with learning that encompasses participation from both students and the educator. One such pedagogical approach, which has been popular for over a decade and that extensively uses active learning methodology, is flipped learning. Pierce and Fox (2012) argue that "[q]uality, not necessarily the quantity, of student-teacher interaction is a compelling force in improving student performance. The flipped classroom provides this through active learning during class" (Pierce & Fox, 2012). The Flipped learning Pedagogical approach boasts of the learning outcomes of students to be of a higher level, enabling them to apply, analyze, and critically evaluate concepts, thus giving them more practical skills for the workforce rather than just giving them knowledge of theoretical aspects. It also develops other important soft skills, such as communicating effectively, collaboratively working in teams, and being reflective, digitally skilled and life-long self-learners (Aronson & Arfstrom, 2013).

As per the definition adopted by the Flipped Learning Global Initiative (FLGI) which was ratified and adopted by the group of all 100 experienced flipped learning educators from 49 countries, when the non-profit *Academy of Active Learning Arts and Sciences* organized a gathering,

*Flipped learning is a framework that enables educators to reach every student. The flipped approach inverts the traditional classroom model by introducing course concepts before class, allowing educators to use class time to guide each student through active, practical, innovative applications of the course principles.*

The interest in flipped learning is evident as indicated by a simple Google search for the term "flipped learning" resulting in 26,600,000 hits, and a Google scholar search resulting in 164,000 hits as of January 2020. The growing number of studies documents "measurable improvements in student and teacher motivation, increased attendance in class and better grades as a result of using the flipped approach" (Ahmed, 2016). However, this interest in flipped learning has not been thoroughly assessed in terms of pedagogy in higher education. There are examples, however, of recording measurable improvements in the test scores of students enrolled in physics flipped classes in 2011 by Vanderbilt University in the US (Deslauriers et al., 2011); the successful implementation of flipped learning for a range of disciplines by the University of Queensland, Australia in 2012-13, which also lead a global partnership of universities in an initiative to better understand how engineering education might be redesigned using the flipped learning model and how the spread and adoption of best practice in flipped learning could be accelerated (University of Queensland 2014); experimenting with the "flipping" of tutorials to be watched in advance through video with tutorial time used for small group work that included problem-based learning activities which eventually resulted in improved student engagement at the University of Manchester, UK (University of Manchester 2014). US universities and schools were the foremost adopters of the flipped model, followed by this concept being tried in Australia and the UK. The MEF, a private university in Istanbul, Turkey, claims to be the first in the world to have adopted flipped learning as pedagogical model for all its programs offered at the university from 2014 onwards and now it is promoting it to others to use it, citing their success as an example (The

World's First "Flipped Learning" University to Host Global Standards Summit, 2018). In India, a private college, JISCE in Kalyani, Kolkata, claims to be the first to have begun their tryst with flipped learning in the middle of 2016 and adopting it as pedagogy for their academic programs, which will see its first batch of students graduating in 2020 (Mukherjee, 2017).

Even though flipped learning has been around for almost a decade now, there is hardly any existing research published on it in India. Many teachers and administrators of higher education in India are still not aware of the concept, with many confusing it to be the same as blended learning. Only a few educators seem to have experimented with it as a tool for teaching, and only a few times. Bakhru (2018) conducted a study on a sample of 336 students from Indian universities and noted the following: "The students' need is changing and the learning methods should change accordingly. Students want to be involved in active learning for which the learning outcomes should be aligned with the teaching and learning methods" (Kanupriya Misra Bakhru, 2018). Some universities do provide facilities for recording video lecture, which are used for blended learning, but none has systems in place to offer flipped learning, except the aforementioned sole example of the private college JISCE in India.

The IAMAI Report 2019 on the Internet in India notes that "India is becoming one of the largest consumers of Internet data globally with close to 451 million Internet users today" (*IAMAI Report*, 2019). With the Indian government's massive Digital India Project and various reports projecting surmounting increases in Internet subscribers, the future educational ecosystem is conducive to the use of the information communication technology (ICT) as a strategy for the improvement of the present status of institutions, which can be done through the adoption and implementation of flipped learning.

Thus, it is timely to explore the current status and use of flipped learning pedagogy in the educational institutes of higher education in India and to find what may be the challenges and opportunities if flipped learning pedagogy is implemented for higher education there. Accordingly, a policy measure/framework will be proposed for effective implementation as an outcome of this research study.

## 1.2 Research Objectives

The flipped learning model has the capacity to equip 21st century learners with necessary skills and attitudes (Lee et al., 2017). Teachers and educators can be considered as front line implementers of this model, thus making it vital to understand their role in and capability to accomplish the implementation of this model, as well as their limitations/challenges. Thus, the research objectives for this study are as follows.

i. **To review the key concepts of flipped learning and its evolvement**

   The key concepts will be reviewed by doing an extensive literature review on the historical background and chronological development of flipped learning, and various research studies carried out on flipped learning and flipped classrooms, especially those focusing on higher education.

ii. **To explore the applications of flipped learning pedagogy in higher education in India.**

   Interviews with several educators, directors, and vice chancellors of institutes of higher education, and some key persons involved in education governance, were done in order to explore the application of flipped learning pedagogy in higher education in India. Field visits were made to the only college that has implemented the flipped learning pedagogy for its entire academic program offerings with an expectation that it would provide an opportunity to gather comprehensive understanding of implementing flipped learning in the Indian context.

iii. **To outline key drivers for adopting flipped learning by educators**

With the understanding gathered from the college visit and interviews, a focus group discussion was conducted with educators from different institutes of higher learning across the India in order to outline the key drivers as well as the challenges experienced or perceived by them in implementing the flipped learning pedagogy. This helped to deeply understand the issues concerned that lead to developing a questionnaire survey. The primary data were then collected from educators of higher education institutes in India on their experiences or perceptions of the use of flipped learning. Factor analysis was then performed on the data collected on the key drivers for implementing flipped learning in higher education in India.

iv. **To identify the challenges in the adoption of flipped learning in higher education in India.**

Flipped learning has become popular over the past decade, and it is beneficial in many ways for students who are the future workforce. Still it has not been adopted as the pedagogy in Indian higher educational institutes. A focus group discussion was held with educator members from different institutes of higher learning from across India to identify the challenges experienced or perceived by them in implementing flipped learning pedagogy. This also helped in further gaining understanding of the issues form the educators point of view that was used in the development of a questionnaire survey for collecting data from educators of higher education institutes in India on their experience or perception of the use of flipped learning.

v. **To model the challenges of a potential framework for the effective implementation of flipped learning in India**

As of now, Indian education policy does not have a comprehensive policy measure/framework for the effective implementation of flipped learning pedagogy in institutes of higher learning in the country. The data collected through the case study of the college that has implemented flipped learning for its academic programs, interviews of educators and administrators, focus group discussion with educators from various universities in India, and the questionnaire survey were analyzed to come up with the factors that influence the effective implementation of flipped learning pedagogy in higher education in India, and a flipped learning framework will be developed using a Total Interpretative Structure Model.

## 1.3 Research Gaps

The vast amount of papers published over the last ten years have been in the areas of exploring the concept of the flipped classroom and learning; the learning outcomes of the students who have undergone learning through flipped teaching in comparison to traditional teaching; and further subject-wise comparisons by setting up quasi-experiments between two different set of students – those taught in a traditional way and others taught using the flipped classroom. Evaluation methods have mostly been limited to quantitative data drawn from course assessments and surveys, and there is a scarcity in qualitative research in terms of understanding the phenomena of flipped learning pedagogy in depth and within specific contexts. There are very few research studies from the educators' perspective of flipped learning – their experiences, their interpretations of learning and teaching skills growth, learning and teaching strategies, challenges and barriers to the implementation, execution, and application of flipped learning, and their strengths and needs as flipped learners or educators. Thus, this research will focus on educators' experiences with and perceptions of flipped learning and the issues and challenges they face if they want to use this type of learning.

Interviews with top administrators and educators, a case study of an institute that uses flipped learning pedagogy, and the data collected through questionnaire survey would be crucial to the understanding of the issues and challenges faced by educators.

## 1.4 Research Questions

This research study seeks to answer the following questions, specifically in context of institutes of higher education in India:

i. If the flipped learning pedagogical approach is supposedly the future of education based on the various studies done and conclusions are positive regarding this approach, then why it has not been adopted across the academic programs offered by institutes of higher learning in India?

ii. What are the challenges/impediments that educators and students face when using the flipped learning approach, especially in case of India?

iii. What resources and support would educators need in transitioning their classroom to a flipped classroom?

iv. If it is proven to positively impact student learning outcomes, then what kind of policy framework should there be at the institute level to scale up the adoption of flipped learning pedagogy by institutes of higher education in India?

## 1.5 Scope of the Study

For this explorative study, the focus is to explore the application of flipped learning pedagogy in the institutes/universities/colleges of higher education in India. Furthermore, rather than comparing the learning outcomes of the students under traditional versus flipped learning for particular courses (research that has already been extensively done), the focus will be to understand the perspectives of the educators/instructors teaching in India with regards to adopting or not adopting flipped learning as a pedagogy, what challenges/impediments they face, and the support/policy measures they need in order to successfully implement it.

## 1.6 Significance of the Study

Though flipped learning has become a widely used approach in higher education teaching worldwide, the educational institutions in India are yet to embrace the concept of flipped learning on a wider scale. The outcomes of this study can be used to introduce flipped learning approach across the country, considering its potential in enhancing the learning experience of students. Study findings and recommendations will help educational institutions in making policy changes related to teaching and learning.

## 1.7 Organization of the Research

The objectives outline for this study would require applying mixed-methods research methodology, with both qualitative and quantitative data collection. The objective 1: "To explore key concepts of flipped learning pedagogy and its evolvement" would be achieved through the literature review. Following this the objective 2: "To explore application of flipped learning pedagogy in higher education in India" would be achieved by conducting interviews, case study of a college in India which has implemented flipped learning pedagogy for all its academic programs since 2016, and finally the focus group discussion with educators from India. This also led to the development of questionnaire survey to collect primary data from educators of various institutes across India. The factor analysis was applied to the primary data collected to achieve objective 3: "To identify key drivers for adoption of flipped learning pedagogy." The objective 4: "To identify challenges faced by educators was achieved through focus group discussion and primary data from questionnaire survey. Finally, the objective 5: "To come up with framework for effective implementation of flipped learning pedagogy" was achieved by applying TISM (the Total interpretative structural modeling). The Figure 1.1 shows the organization of the research.

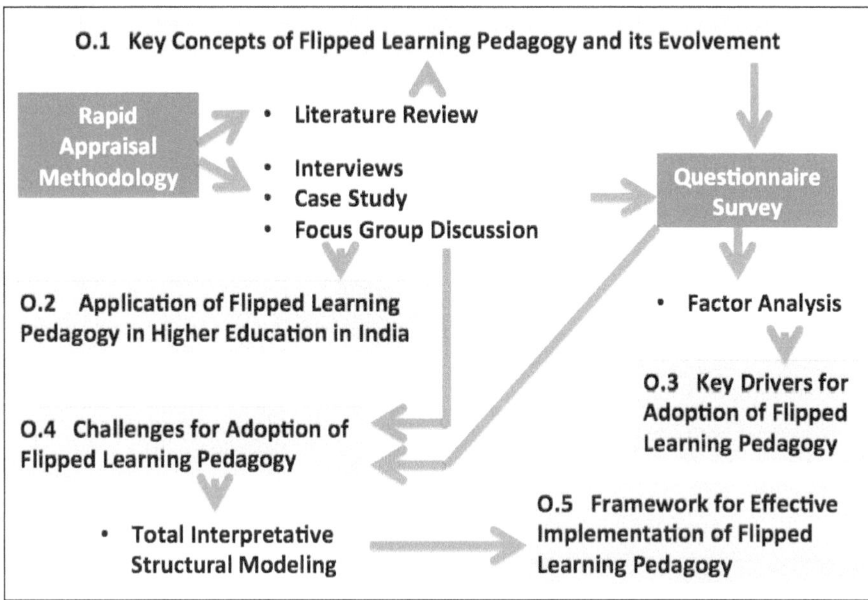


**Figure 1.1** Organization of the Research

## Chapter 2

# CONTEXT

*"A teacher can never truly teach unless he is still learning himself. A lamp can never light another lamp unless it continues to burn its own flame. The teacher who has come to the end of his subject, who has no living traffic with his knowledge but merely repeats his lesson to his students, can only load their minds, he cannot quicken them."*

– ***Rabindranath Tagore***
*(Nobel Prize in Literature in 1913)*

The starting point of the literature review was the book "Flip Your Classroom" by Jonathan Bergmann and Aaron Sams, published in 2012 (Sams & Washington, 2012). This book is always cited in any article, news, and research paper published related to flipped learning and the search with key words including the flipped classroom, flipped learning, blended learning, inverted learning, active learning, digital pedagogy, etc. This can be considered as the bible of the flipped learning approach and the authors impress the reader through their experiences with flipping high school chemistry classes. The concept of flipping classroom lectures with video lectures online began with concern for students who had missed their classes due to their participation in sports and other important activities, or because of illness, were unable to catch up in understanding the portion of the subject already taught in class. Bergmann and Sams experimented by recording their lectures on video, uploading them for students to view them for self-study, and discuss with teachers for clearing up any doubts. They found that not just the students who had missed the class, but other students as well who had repetitively watched videos on their own, demonstrated improvements in their performance, evident by their grades in the subject. This made the authors realize the potential of video lectures to be covered at home prior to class, and utilizing the lecture time for interactive sessions and solving problems in class. They began to give talks about their experience and raised awareness about this teaching and learning approach, and several others began to report their similar experiences. From this point onwards flipped learning began to become popular amongst educators and researchers.

In addition to the book cited above, several other books and book chapters were reviewed by the present author for understanding the evolvement of the flipped learning pedagogy. Finally, selected research publications in the past decade in journals were reviewed for further exploring the concept of the flipped learning, especially those focusing on higher education, with further narrowing down to its application and implementation in India for the higher education. Though there is not much literature available in India on this topic, international research publications were reviewed, which could be later applied and compared in the Indian context.

This provided the necessary background knowledge on the flipped learning approach and the various models being used. The search for relevant literature was done using key words, such as flipped learning, flipped classroom, inverted classroom, active learning, blended learning, and relevant journal publications since 2008 were also reviewed. The classic book on flipped learning mentioned above was reviewed along with several other books on topics or chapters in books that are detailed in the literature review.

Kaushik (2016) in Chapter 5 entitled 'Technology Supported Pedagogy in Higher Education: Approaches and Trends' from Raman (2016) book "Emerging Trends in Higher Education Pedagogy" notes that the easily available and affordable global digital connectivity with improved access, quality, and interactivity has compelled the academicians and educators to utilize them to the advantage of the learner populace, as a consequence of which pedagogical approaches and supportive applications are evolving to fit with the changing times (Raman, 2016). Flipped learning is one amongst other noticeable developments in pedagogy, such as blended learning, MOOCs, Web 2.0 Supported Pedagogies, crowd learning, etc. Making decision to adopt particular pedagogical approach by the educator depends on the requirements and competences of the educators as well as the readiness of the institute in terms of providing incentives, resources, and infrastructure.

Many research scholars have desired to move into a pedagogical approach that is more active, cooperative, and learner-centered (e.g. Bonwell & Eison 1991; Felder & Brent 2009; Lambert & McCombs 1998; as cited in Sale and Cheah 2017). However, still lecture-based teaching continues to be the primary method used worldwide, with few educators being comfortable using the flipped learning approach. While the flipped learning approach is easily understood concept, it is not easy to implement it due to "the range of technical skills, conceptual knowledge, and pedagogical expertise required executing varying aspects of the method" (Shimamoto, 2012). It has been further cautioned that implementing the flipped learning approach without proper preparation can result in unexpected repercussions across the subject content and delivery (Newton & Hes 2013).

The core of flipped learning is using active learning in the classroom, which can address the above-mentioned challenges. As per The CDIO™ Initiative, an innovative educational framework for producing the next generation of engineers, the Standard 8 "Active Learning" notes the following: "Active learning methods engage students directly in thinking and problem solving activities. There is less emphasis on passive transmission of information rather more on engaging students in manipulating, applying, analyzing, and evaluating ideas. Active learning is considered experiential when students take on roles that simulate professional engineering practice, for example, design-implement projects, simulations, and case studies." The flipped classroom also fits well with the rationale for Standard 8 "By engaging students in thinking about concepts, particularly new ideas and requiring them to make an overt response, students not only learn more, they recognize for themselves what and how they learn. This process helps to increase students' motivation to achieve program learning outcomes and form habits of lifelong learning. With active learning methods, instructors can help students make connections among key concepts and facilitate the application of this knowledge to new settings."

In their review of flipped classroom implementation, O'Flaherty and Phillips (2015) highlighted that the "key obstacle for educator in designing, implementing and evaluating the effectiveness of their flipped classrooms is a lack of pedagogical understanding of how to effectively translate the flipped classroom concept into practice" (O'Flaherty & Phillips, 2015). Hamdan, McKnight, and Arfstrom (2013) argued that "teachers do recognize the value of using sound pedagogical approaches to enhance the student experiences through curriculum renewal, but need support to develop skills needed to effectively guide the systematic use of technologies and translate conceptual thinking into planned learning sequences" (Hamdam et al., 2013).

## 2.1 Key Concepts of Flipped Learning Pedagogy and Its Evolvement

### 2.1.1 Historical Background

In the early mid-2000s, the term flipped learning became a buzzword and was propagated by chemistry teachers Jon Bergman and Aaron Sams (Bergmann & Sams, 2014) through their book "Flip Your Classroom," and the founder of the Khan Academy, Salman Khan, through his Ted Talk "Technology, Entertainment, Design Talk" with the phrase "Flip Your Class" (TED 2011). However, flipped learning can be trailed back to 1990s, when Harvard professor Eric M Mazur developed a model for "peer instruction." As per Mazur's theory, "if information transfer could be taken out of the classroom, then more time could be spent within the classroom on student- centered, information assimilation activities that apply the learning" (Mazur, 2014). Mazur believes that peer instruction facilitates student learning most effectively.

In 2012, various educators promoting flipped learning, such as Jon Bergmann, Aaron Sams, April Gudenrath, Kristin Daniels, Troy Cockrum, Brian Bennett and others jointly launched a non-profit organization called the "Flipped Learning Network," which later in 2016 was renamed the "Flipped Learning Global Community." "This network presents both pedagogical and best-practice consultation and discussions, in addition to practical and pragmatic support on technology and implementation" (Ahmed, 2016).

The term flipped or flipping seems to have been first used by Wesley Baker in 2000 during academic research on learning management system. This was followed by Tenneson and McGlasson in 2006, who shared with other educators their experience of flipping a course when they applied blended learning using technology to flip a class that provided more time for active discussion (Tenneson, 2006). Then in 2007, Jeremy Strayer, during his research for his doctoral studies, compared student's learning activities in the traditional versus flipped classroom that used an intelligent tutoring system, and he then continued his research on the impact of inverted (flipped) learning on cooperation, innovation, and task orientation, which he published in 2012 (J. Strayer, 2007; J. F. Strayer, 2012).

Some of the initial educators who tried the flipped classroom and noted improved student learning were McConnell and Steer in mathematics, Owens in geology in 2003, Chew in psychology in 2004, Smith in biology in 2009, and Simon, Kohanfars, Lee, Tamayo, and Cutts for computer science in 2010. Then in 2013, Harvard professor, Margo Seltzer, flipped her computer engineering operating systems class, which saw greater student engagement with attendance going up by 75 percent, and students reporting the efficacy of this approach including for the struggling students and a sense of community (Zhan & Mei,

2013). During the same year, an extraordinary drop in the failure rate of students across all subject areas was noted when the flipped classroom was introduced at a high school in Clintondale, US, which eventually adopted a flipped teaching model in 2011 (Rosenberg, 2013), and similarly showed an increase of 46 percent in the pass rate in an electrical engineering course at California State University flipped (Ferenstein, 2013, as cited by Fell Kurban 2015).

Various magazines and newspapers began to write articles, such as *The New York Times* citing the example of online learning being used effectively by a professor at Stanford (Keller, 2011), and an article entitled "Classroom Lectures Go Digital" (Fitzpatrick, 2012). *The Chronicle of Higher Education* had a article entitled "How Flipping the Classroom Can Improve the Traditional Lecture" (Berrett, 2012), and *Harvard Magazine* published an article called "Twilight of the Lecture - The trend toward 'active learning' may overthrow the style of teaching that has ruled universities for 600 years" (Lambert, 2012); and *The Stanford Daily* in December 2012 printed an article entitled "Flipped Classroom Movement Gains Steam" (Gifford, 2012). To conclude, flipped learning has evolved over the last decade and has become popular amongst educators and researchers, especially in the west where access to technology with high Internet speed is not an issue, which is the main footing for flipped learning.

### 2.1.2 The Concept of Flipped Learning

Traditionally, educators through the delivery of lectures disseminate the knowledge during the class session. The students in this set up mostly are passive listeners, though they can ask questions for clarification. The students need to take notes while listening to the lectures in order to memorize, the knowledge gained and to use it for higher cognitive activities involving applying, analyzing, and evaluating. This traditional approach has inherent weaknesses, with a focus on content delivery rather than student having access to the instructor or peer support when needed most, while undertaking higher level of applying and analyzing problems.

The time of both educator as well as student is not used effectively in the traditional learning. The "flipping" of this learning process overcomes the weaknesses encountered in the traditional set up.

Flipped learning has been defined in various ways by different educators, which suggests that it has evolved over time. For Stone (2012) it is "a learning model in which the students watch related videos before the course and spend course time to learn the complex issues, answer the questions and establish connections with everyday life situations" (Stone, 2012). Similarly for Murray, Koziniec and McGill (2015) it is "a learning approach in which students learn basic knowledge through short videos at home and come to the classroom environment to understand the situations that they have difficulty in learning and correct misunderstandings" (Murray et al., 2015). The function of the videos here can be considered as a tool for disseminating the course content as well as being used as a digital leaning platform (McNeill & Bardsley, 2016). For Gopalan and Klann (2017) it is "a blended educational model that allows student-centered learning in the classroom by moving teacher-guided learning out of the classroom" (Gopalan & Klann, 2017).

Some educators however feel that the course content prior to class should not be limited to video lectures or content sourced from Internet, which can also be attained by appropriate learning materials and guidance (M. K. Kim et al. 2014). Taking this into consideration, the flipped learning can be defined as "a learning model in which the students learn the course's content by using video, presentation, written documents, etc. benefiting from the technological opportunities before the course, and learn more deeply in the classroom by the help of discussion, question-answer and practical activities through the reinforcement, questioning and application of the background knowledge" (Kozikoğlu, 2019).

In 2018, the definition of the flipped learning was ratified and adopted unanimously by a group of 100 experienced Flipped learning educators from 49 countries when the non-profit *Academy of Active Learning Arts and Sciences* organized a gathering, and that has now been also adopted by the Flipped learning Global Initiative (FLGI) (*Flipped Learning Global Initiative*, 2018), as can be seen in the following:

> *Flipped learning is a framework that enables educators to reach every student. The flipped approach inverts the traditional classroom model by introducing course concepts before class, allowing educators to use class time to guide each student through active, practical, innovative applications of the course principles.*

Dr. Robert Talbert, a math Professor at Grand Valley State University, in Michigan in the US, and a regular blogger on flipped learning, used a metaphor to describe flipped learning: "Think of flipped as the operating system of education. All the other active-learning strategies, such as project-based learning, inquiry and mastery learning—those are the apps. Flipped is a framework to make this all work".

In simple words, the traditional lecture delivery in classroom is flipped with the related assignments/projects/group discussions taking place outside classroom. The students are introduced to the learning material prior to class, thus allowing class time to be used more efficiently in order to deepen the students' understanding through discussion with peers and problem-solving activities facilitated by teachers. The students engage in active learning rather than being just passive listeners in a one- way knowledge flow, from teacher to students. Lectures can be in form of materials such as course videos and soft files in various formats, including PowerPoint slides prepared by educators, Excel files, PDFs, and images made available to students online prior to class through a learning management system (LMS) such as Moodle, Blackboard, etc.

The flipped learning system fits seamlessly with the Bloom Taxonomy (see Figure-2.1), with the students performing lower-level cognitive tasks such as learning and understanding on their own outside and prior to class (which under the traditional system is done in class) and higher-level cognitive tasks such as practice, analysis, synthesis and evaluation being performed along with educator and peer support during class hours. The

Bloom Taxonomy depicts the levels of learning moving upwards from remembering to understading-applying-analyzing-evaluating-creating (remembering being at the lowest level and creating being at the peak point). In Traditioanal Learning, the teachers transmit content for lower levels of remembering, understanding and applying in classroom, with higher-level learning of analyzing, evaluating, and creating left for students' independent study – the time when they need most support. This gets inverted in the flipped learning with the three lower levels of learning performed by students independently prior to class and the three higher levels of learning performed in class together with the educator and all students, thus enabling the students to receive needed support at the crucial level of learning.

It is important to emphasize that flipping a class can, but does not necessarily, lead to flipped learning. Many educators may already flip their classes by having students read text outside of class, watching supplemental videos, or solving additional problems, but to engage in flipped learning, educators must incorporate the "Four pillars of F-L-I-P" into their practice as elaborated along with the eleven indicators seen in Figure-2.2. The focus of this study is the last pillar, the professional educator in the context of higher education in India, where the educators have been slow to adopt this pedagogical method for teaching.

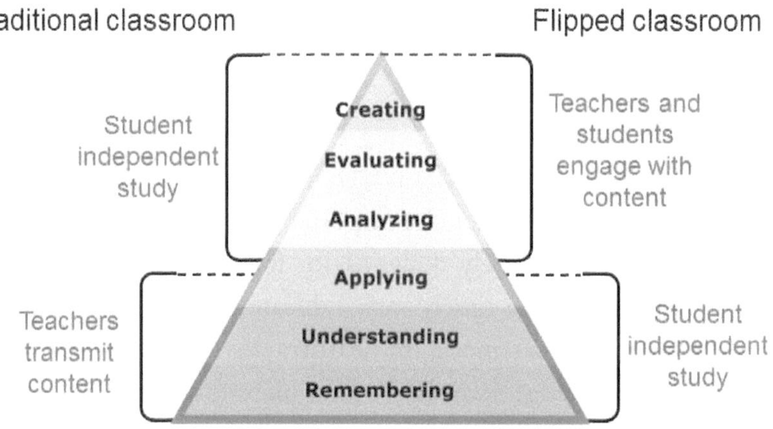


**Figure 2.1** The Flipped Classroom and Bloom's Taxonomy

*(Source: profkinchinblog.wordpress.com)*

The promoters of flipped learning advocate a shift from a teacher-centered to a student-centric learning ecosystem, including blended, dynamic, and collaborative learning provisions where students are intensely absorbed in their learning. Thus the shift from "sage on the stage" to "guide on the side" is emphasized and considered as vital factor for flipped learning (Baker 2000, Bergmann and Sams 2014). However, many educators while possibly having the skills to develop student-centered learning content suitable for flipped learning, may not have the training or experience to put this into effect in the classroom (Ahmed, 2016).

The education ecosystem for the flipped learning approach requires three major role players – the students, educators, and content as mentioned below:

i. The role of the students is to be responsible for their own learning, thus studying themselves the materials provided in greater depth prior to the class and also collaborate with peers. Furthermore, they need to actively participate in class in order to enhance their knowledge in a meaningful learning environment (Sams & Washington, 2012).

ii. The role of the educator is to shift his/her role from "sage on the stage" to "guide on the side." Thus, the educator cannot merely rely on disseminating limited knowledge but must also be able to acquire it from learners. The class time has to be utilized in active learning by facilitating and mentoring, as well as advising and providing feedback on each learner's progress. The educator's role becomes all the more important in preparing course content that is appropriately designed for flipped learning and making it accessible in a timely way. Educators also need to "create an alternative assessment for learners to elicit and demonstrate their knowledge according to the prescribed learning outcomes" (Bergmann & Sams, 2014).

iii. The role of the content is to enable students to acquire knowledge from suitably designed content for flipped learning, such as videos and content in the form of articles, advertisements, movies, songs, TV broadcasts, newspapers, magazines, etc. : "The videos, in this case, are great learning tool for learners in order to help them learn at their own pace outside of classroom" (Bergmann & Sams, 2014).

## The Four Pillars of FLIPTM

| F Flexible Environment | | |
|---|---|---|
| Flipped Learning allows for a variety of learning modes: educators often physically rearrange their learning spaces to accommodate a lessor or unit, to support either group work or independent study. They create flexible spaces in which students chooses when and where they learn. Furthermore, educators who flip their classes are flexible in their expectations of student timelines for learning and in their assessments of student learning | F.1 | □ I establish spaces and time frames that permit sutdents to interact and reflect on their learning as needed. |
| | F.2 | □ I continuously observe and observe and monitor students to make adjustments as appropriate |
| | F.3 | □ I provide students withdifferent ways to learn content and demonstrate mastery |

| L Learning Culture | | |
|---|---|---|
| In the traditional teacher-centered model, the teacher is the primary source of information. By contrast, the Flipped Learning model deliberately shifts instruction to a learner-centered approach, where in-class time is dedicated to exploring topics in greater depth and creating rich learning opportunities. As a result, students are actively involved in knowledge construction as they particiapate in and evaluate their learning in a manner that is personally meaningful. | L.1 | □ I give students opportunities to engage in meaningful activities without the teacher being central. |
| | L.2 | □ I scaffold these activities and make them accessible to all students through differentiation and feedback. |

| I Intentional Content | | |
|---|---|---|
| Flipped Learning Educators continually think about how they can use the Flipped Learning model to help students develop conceptual understanding, as well as procedural fluency. They determine what they need to teach and what materials students should explore on their own. Educators use Intentional Content to maximize classroom time in order to adopt methods of student-centered, active learning strategies, depending on grade level and subject matter | I.1 | □ I prioritize concepts used in direct instruction for learners to access on their own. |
| | I.2 | □ I create and/or curate relevant content (typically videos) for my students. |
| | I.3 | □ I differentiate to make content accessible and relevant to all students. |

| P Professional Educator | | |
|---|---|---|
| The role of a Professional Educator is even more important, and often more demanding, in a Flipped Classroom than in a traditional one. During class time, they continually observe their students, providing them with feedback relevant in the moment, and assessing their work. Professional Educators are reflective in their practice, connec with each other to improve their instruction, accept constructive criticism, and tolerate controlled chaos in their classrooms. While Professional Educators take on less visibly prominent roles in a flipped classroom, they remain the essential ingredient that enables Flipped Learning to occur. | P.1 | □ I make myself available to students for individual, small group, and class feedback in real time as needed. |
| | P.2 | □ I conduct ongoing formative assessments during class time through observation and recording data to inform future instruction. |
| | P.3 | □ I collaborate and reflect wih other educators and take responsibiltiy for transforming my practice. |

**Figure 2.2** Four Pillars of F-L-I-PTM

*Source: Flipped Learning Network (FLN) (2014). The Four Pillars of F-L-I-P*[TM]

Flipped learning can be divided into three phases: the knowledge delivery, knowledge internalization, and knowledge consolidation, as shown in Figure-2.3 (He et al., 2019). However, all phases comprise of active engagement of the educator as well as learners/peers in a facilitative environment organically processing and disseminating ideas and concepts, with the main emphasis on deeper learning strategies, peer discussions, and enhancing problem-solving techniques.

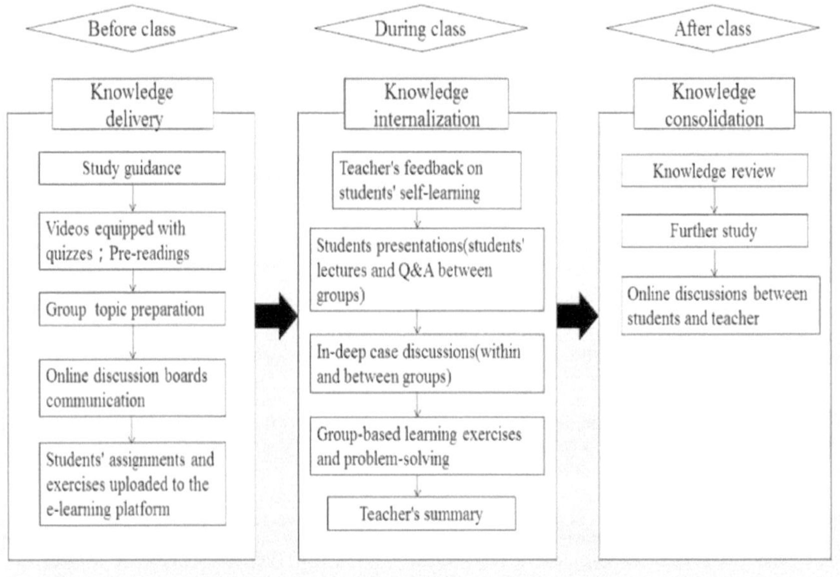


**Figure 2.3** The Flipped Classroom structure and Setting flowchart

*Source: https://doi.org/10.1371/journal.pone.0214624.g001*

A paper published in the ICERI 2014 in the 7th International Conference of Education, Research and Innovation lists the advantages and disadvantages of flipped classrooms, as seen below (Ramirez et al., 2014).

**Benefits:**

i. Students can allocate more time to study content at an individual pace and preferred time in accordance with their learning style.

ii. Learners are engaged and build their own study plan as per their study progress.

iii. The social skills and teamwork spirit of students develop and improve due to the active learning environment where they need to cooperate and collaborate with their peers and become involved in group work.

iv. It results in improved learning outcomes of students.

v. It improves interaction with teacher during lecture session.

vi. Appropriate learning resources are build such as recorded lectures, video on- screen demonstrations of certain software, and additional resources from video sharing platforms.

vii. Students can learn continuously despite the absence of the educator or self- absence due to participation in other activities or due to illness.

**Limitations:**

i. It might not be suitable for all subjects.

ii. There can be Internet accessibility limitations.

iii. Both educator and student have to put extra effort into learning process that requires active participation. With the liberty that student gets in this system, they need to be more responsible.

iv. Educators have to be techno-savvy, which enables them to create resources for online delivery of lectures or teaching contents and also to develop class sessions utilizing active learning strategies.

Further, the advantages and disadvantages of flipped learning can be summed up as indicated in Table 2.1.

**Table 2.1** Advantages vs. Disadvantages of Flipped Learning

| Advantages | Disadvantages |
|---|---|
| • Students take ownership for learning<br>• Lessons and contents are accessible anytime<br>• Promotes student-centered learning<br>• Encourages critical thinking<br>• Strengthens teamwork and co-operative skills<br>• Efficient allowing for more time to explore the topic<br>• Continuous evaluation of student learning rather<br>• than waiting for mid-term or final exam results | • Possible digital divide<br>• Depends on preparation<br>• Additional work for educators<br>• Additional work for students |

## 2.1.3 Misconceptions about Flipped Learning

The flipped learning concept is quiet simple, but still misconceptions about this pedagogical approach exist even after its popularity and the awareness created over the past decade. The prevalent misunderstanding is that the role of the educator is substituted or minimized by the videos when the flipped learning method is used. Salman Khan, who runs Khan Academy with a goal to provide "a free world-class education to anyone anywhere" through its more than 4,000 repository videos, stated that on the contrary, the educator has a superior role requiring the conducting of interactive learning activities at advanced levels with students, monitoring students individually as well as in a groups, and administering peer-to-peer learning (Khan, 2011).

The other issue is the confusion created due to the use of online course being common in the case of both flipped and blended learning. Both the online learning or blended learning will remain integral part of education field, but it should not be cluttered with the flipped learning which in no way changes the amount of time student spends in class interacting with educator when compared to the traditional classroom (Ahmed, 2016). This misconception seems to be the case amongst Indian educators as well, which surfaced during the interviews and focus group discussion conducted by the present researcher, and in a paper where an Indian educator has noted his experience with flipped course in an Indian university, which as per the modalities explained in the paper clearly indicates that it was actually blended learning that was used and not flipped learning. In this same paper, while noting that "[a]dopting the flipped method is very useful for a country like India that has a large number of students to be educated, simultaneously with a shortage of good teachers and curricular material," the author has referred to two papers that are actually on distance learning and not flipped learning. The infographic in Figure 2.4, from the Innovative Learning Institute, demonstrates clearly that flipped learning can be considered as part of a blended learning environment, but the blended learning environment need not necessarily have a flipped learning environment.

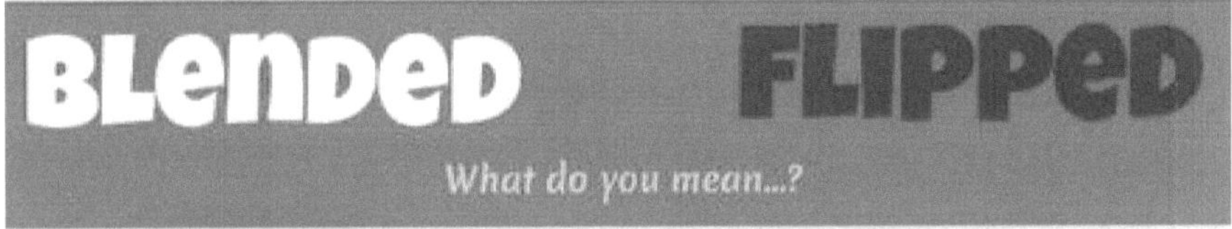

Two of the hottest trends in technology enhanced teaching and learning are blended learning and the flipped classroom. Each model is effective, yet they are distinctly different approaches. If you get confused about which is which, think of this formulation... all flipped classroom courses are blended courses, but not all blended courses are flipped classroom courses

## BLENDED

A Blended Learning course is one in which a portion of in-class time is replaced by online activities. For example, a small group discussion takes place in an online format rather than in class. The online activities allow for individual reflection as well as collaborative learning among students.

## FLIPPED

The Flipped Classroom is one in which traditional in-class activity—the lecture—is delivered outside of class . In-class time is used for small group problem-solving, and other such activities that allow students to engage at a deep level with the content they viewed outside of (and before) class.

## WHY USE THE BLENDED LEARNING MODEL?

The blended learning model has been known to:

<Give students time to reflect

<Empower every student to participate and be "visible"

<Enable the instructor to provide oversight and feedback "anywhere, anytime"

## WHY USE THE FLIPPED CLASSROOM MODEL?

The flipped classroom model has been known to:

<Enable instructors to help students who struggle most

<Allow students to pause and rewind the video lectures as needed

<Empower students and instructors to have frequent and substantial interactions

A common challenge for both models is the "course and a half syndrome" which is the tendency for instructors to add blended or flipped classroom components without reducing other components accordingly. Another common challenge is motivating students to complete the out-of-class activities; the online discussions and the video assignments.

**Figure 2.4** Flipped vs. Blended

*Source: From https://mrmck.wordpress.com/tag/blended-learning/*

## 2.2 Theoretical Frameworks

The role of the educator and learner is altered in the flipped learning environment, with the educator becoming a catalyst for the student's learning and with students becoming self-directed learners reclaiming the lessons at their individual space through Edmodo, YouTube, Google Apps, Dropbox, Educreation, GlogsterEdu, Screencast, Socrative, Teaching Channel, Twitter, etc. (Ahmed, 2016). The flipped learning, with its basis in the student-centered approach, all theories that focus on student-centered learning are relevant for this approach. The Figure-2.5 shows Venn diagram with student-centered theories.

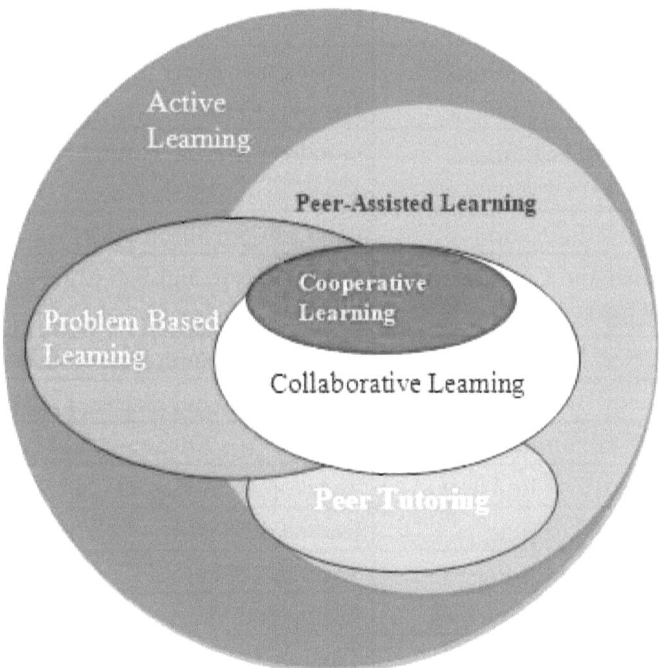


**Figure 2.5** Venn Diagram of Student-centered Learning Theories and Methods

*Source: Adopted from Makinde (2017)*

Karabulut-Ilgu et al. in their research article noted the following: "The synthesis of 62 publications on flipped learning studied revealed that only 13 publications had referred to a theoretical or conceptual framework". This research articles provided a Table with theoretical frameworks cited by various authors in addition to the Constructivist Theory and Bloom Taxonomy that fits with flipped learning well. The Table 2.2 given here is extended table including other authors who have used some other theoretical frameworks that matches with the flipped learning approach. (Karabulut-Ilgu et al., 2018).

**Table 2.2** Theoretical Frameworks Cited in Studies

| ***Theoretical Framework*** | ***Studies*** |
|---|---|
| • Bloom Taxonomy for Cognitive Learning | Bloom (1949) later revised in (2001) |
| • Transactional Theory | Chen, Wang, Kinshuk, and Chen (2014) |
| • The Thayer System | Chetchui, Hans, and Brent (2014) |
| • Problem-based Learning & Collaborative Learning | Chiang and Wang (2015)<br>Barrow (1996) |
| • Collaborative Learning | Goodsell, Maher, Tinto, Smith, & MacGregor (1992) |
| • Cooperative Education | Choi (2013), Slavin (1991) |
| • Traditional and Constructivist Approaches | Davies, Dean, and Bali (2013) |
| • Team-based Learning | Ghadiri, Qayoumi, Junn, and Hsu (2014) |
| • Technology Acceptance Model | Ivala, Thiart, and Gachago (2013) |
| • Revised Community of Inquiry | Kim, Patrick, Srivastava, and Law (2014) |
| • Socio-constructivist Theory | Redekopp and Ragusa (2013) |
| • Self-directed Learning | Rutkowski (2014) |
| • Inquiry-based Learning | Schmidt (2014) |
| • Student-Centered Learning | Bishop and Verleger (2013) |
| • Peer Tutoring | Tabacek, McLaughlin and Howard (1994) |
| • Active Learning | Michael (2006) |
| • Peer Assisted Learning | Topping and Ehly (1998) |

*Source: The Authors British Journal of Educational Technology*

*(Note: The above table is extended using the one cited in "The Authors British Journal of Educational Technology")*

Some examples of theoretical framework applications to flipped learning are:

i. Chetcuti, Hans and Brent (2014) adapted the traditional Thayer System from United States Military Academy to encourage better preparation by students prior to class thereby leaving more time for classroom interactive session.

ii. Kim et al. (2014) adopted the Revised Community of Inquiry (RCOI) model as their analytical framework. This theory establishes existence of cognitive presence, social presence, teaching presence, and learner presence as four important elements required for a successful learning environment.

iii. Chen et al. (2014) added three learning activities – "progressive networking learning activities, engaging and effective learning activities, and diversified and seamless learning platforms" – to the existing four pillars, "Flexible environments, Learning Culture, Intentional Content, and Professional Educators," which was recommended by the Flipped Learning Network (2015) for a more effective course design for flipped learning. The authors have concluded that flipped learning was effective, resulting in high satisfaction among students, increased attendance, and increased study efforts.

iv. Redekopp and Ragusa (2013) found the educator role of facilitator as expert/apprentice in the flipped classroom to be built upon socio-constructivist theory, with learning being a social process where knowledge is co- constructed amongst learners rather than it being transmitted from a knowledgeable person (i.e. educator) to a less knowledgeable person (i.e. learner) (Mayer, 2004).

v. In flipped learning, the educator demonstrates the ways of thinking and solving problems in a given field, and learners follow and improve their learning based on the feedback they receive from the educator. Along these lines, Chiang (2015) and Chao, (2015) adopted frameworks encouraging peer collaboration under the guidance of the educator such as collaborative learning. Choi (2013) and Gannod (2008) adopted cooperative education and Ghadiri, Qayoumi, Junn and Hsu (2014) adopted team-based learning.

vi. Chiang (2015) and Schmidt (2014) found that the flipped learning framework has its root in problem-based learning and inquiry-based learning being constructivist in nature.

vii. Rutkowski (2014) framed flipped learning as a new form of self-directed learning as the students first study the materials on their own using the online materials created by the instructor, and then put that knowledge into practice in the classroom through problem solving with the help of the teacher and peers. The author also concluded that gaining from flipped learning requires learners to have strong determination regarding self-directed learning.

Educators adopt a holistic approach of teaching and learning that enables them to combine direct instruction and in-class active learning with constructivist approaches (Davies et al., 2013). The "Constructivist Theory of Bruner" and "Bloom Taxonomy for Cognitive Learning" are two theories that are repeatedly cited by research scholars as those fitting aptly with the flipped learning. The Constructivism encompasses the idea of learning as an active process, enabling learners to interact and communicate, which motivates learning more effectively than when learners engage in a learning process where they are inactive. In flipped learning, learners watch videos (with content otherwise delivered in class) prior to class, thereby freeing class time for inquiry-based learning that reinforces the principles and notion of constructivism (Brandt, 1997). Flipped learning, backed-up by constructivist theory, "should empower learners to involve in communicating, imaginative and collaborative activities during knowledge construction" (Kim and Bonk 2006). The role of the educator here is to help learners gain knowledge themselves, i.e. in line with constructivist learning theory, where the educator provides the required content and tools for the learners that enable them to develop their creative skills while comprehending the knowledge gained.

Bloom believed that there is a need to focus on learning outcomes that are placed at higher levels in the hierarchy of learning stages, such as problem solving, applying principles, analytical skills, and creativity, and not simply on basic skills such as memorizing and understanding. The rationale is that these abilities stays with the learner, who can utilize them in his or her professional life, without being baffled by the details of the subject matter that was learnt during school times. Additionally, these abilities help to build life-long learning attitude, which is helpful in this ever- changing world (Bloom 1978 cited by Ahmed 2016). Bloom's Taxonomy categorizes various levels of learning, from basic memorizing to applying knowledge to innovating and creating something new. Figure 2.6 depicts the process of learning in the flipped classroom that fits Bloom's Taxonomy.

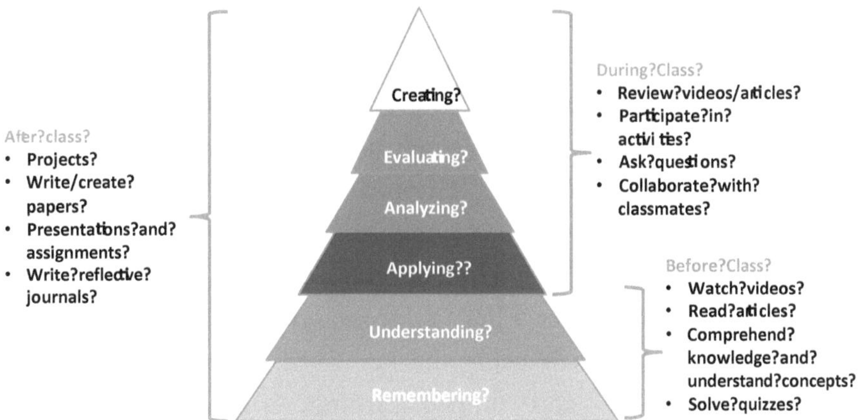


**Figure 2.6** Bloom Taxonomy: Flipped Classroom

Hashemifardnia et al. also cite the cognitive load theory in the context of flipped learning in their paper. According to this theory, learners' "cognitive capacity in working memory is limited, so that if a learning task requires too much capacity, learning will be hampered" (de Jong, 2010). Thus, in order to deepen learning, prior knowledge helps and reduces cognitive load during learning and in retaining knowledge. The authors state that students in the traditional setting receive information on the topic for the first time and their main focus is on listening rather than grasping, which is not possible in the short time available in the classroom. This leads to their inability to absorb information/knowledge to the level at which they feel comfortable and have meaningful discussions (Hashemifardnia et al., 2018). On the other hand, their study suggested that the interaction amongst students in the flipped classroom is esoteric as well as vibrant, and stimulates in-depth thinking and higher- order reasoning.

## 2.3 Rising Interest in Flipped Learning Pedagogy

A math professor at Grand Valley State University, in Michigan in the US, Dr. Robert Talbert, regularly blogs on the topic of flipped learning and has been following research publications on flipped learning since 2000. According to him while the articles/papers on flipped learning began to be published starting in 2000, the research in this area was scanty with few publications a year until 2013. Growth in publication exponentially picked up only around 2012, as indicated in the graph below. Dr. Talbert states that "[f]lipped learning is exciting and the research is still emerging, with idea maturing that needs to be studied as such." Even with the limitation that the graph below (Figure 2.7) is based only on a search using the ERIC database, which was further filtered by peer-reviewed journals using the key words "flipped classrooms," "inverted classrooms," and "flipped learning," it gives a clear idea of the rising interest in the flipped learning. The American Society of

Engineering Education (ASEE) is the most common publication venue. (Karabulut-Ilgu et al., 2018)

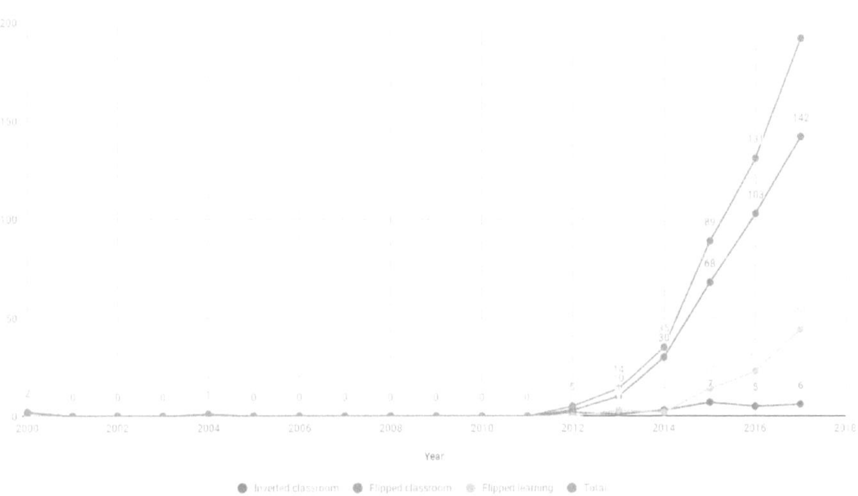


**Figure 2.7** Rise in Published Research on Flipped Learning

*Source: https://rtalbert.org/how-much-research-update/*

## 2.3.1 Research Studies on the Effects of Flipped Learning

The Flipped Learning Network now renamed the Flipped Learning Global Initiative has generated a comprehensive review of research focused on flipped learning. Their findings showed that, in general, educators that apply flipped learning find improved student learning outcomes and attitudes toward learning, and increased student engagement, while educators themselves feel re-energized with personal job satisfaction.

Mostly researchers have deployed experiments by randomly dividing students into experimental (flipped classroom) and control group (traditional classroom). The findings report both beneficial effects as well as no significant effect of the flipped classroom. The positive effects reported are on the students' academic success, attitudes, self-efficacy perceptions, critical thinking skills, and information literacy. Some studies' have reported no significant difference in terms of academic achievement scores.

The beneficial effects reported include the following:

i. Both students and educators having positive perception of the active learning environment experienced in flipped classroom.

ii. Students develop a deeper understanding of the content.

iii. Increased students' motivation for gaining knowledge and feeling satisfied

iv. More active engagement during class with students' participating extensively in discussions, activities, problem solving and group work in a more enjoyable manner

v. Improved achievement on formative/summative assessments

vi. Encourages communication between students and teachers due to the interactive environment in the flipped classroom

vii. Develops reciprocity and cooperation among students

viii. Emphasizes time and deadlines on tasks, thus keeping students more organized

ix. Students can learn more easily with prior knowledge.

Studies conducted in Turkey are presented by Kozikoğlu and some of the findings match with the above listed "positive effects of flipped learning on the students' academic achievement, motivation, meta-cognitive awareness, self-learning ability, attitudes and retention of learning, while at the same time reducing the level of homework/task stress and anxiety". In Kozikoğlu's qualitative study, the positive aspects of flipped learning noted by the educators and students were summarized as "enabling active participation of the students, providing effective and permanent learning, enhancing motivation, providing a fun and positive classroom environment, ensuring flexible and self-paced learning, increasing classroom interaction (sharing), increasing students' responsibility, developing students' higher order thinking skills, providing students with ready access to learning materials, providing students with self-confidence, reducing anxiety" (Kozikoğlu, 2019).

Karabulut-Ilgu et al. synthesized 62 publications on flipped learning, which revealed that most found flipped learning to be more "effective" and "effective and/or no difference," some found it to have "no difference," with very few reporting it to be "less effective" and "less effective and/or no difference" as listed in Table-2.3 (Karabulut-Ilgu et al., 2018).

A similar study was also conducted by research scholars Cheng, Ritzhaupt, and Antonenko (2019) to see the overall effect of the flipped learning environment on student achievements in relation to a set of moderating factors such as student levels, publication types, study durations, and subject area. For this, they searched seventeen databases, out of which 55 relevant publications (published between 2000 and 2016) were selected. Their finding revealed positive attitudes toward the flipped learning environment (Cheng et al., 2019). Other similar meta-analyses conducted around the same time by Chen, Lo, and Hew (2018) found results in favor of flipped learning with improved effects when educators employed quizzes at the beginning of the class session in order to ascertain the students' learning from videos watched prior to the class. They also found improved effect on examination scores (Hew and Lo 2018 cited in Lee and Choi 2018); however, another study by Gillette (2018) indicated no significant difference on final examination scores (Gillette, 2018)

**Table 2.3** Findings on Flipped Learning Effectiveness

| *Findings* | *Studies* |
|---|---|
| Flipped is more effective | Amresh, Carberry, & Femiani (2013); Chao, Chen, and Chuang (2015); Chiang and Wang (2015)*; Fowler (2014); Kalavally, Chan, and Khoo (2014); Lemley *et al.* (2013); Mason, Shuman, and Cook (2013b)*; McGivney-Burelle and Xue (2013); Ossman and Warren (2014)*; Papadopoulos and Roman (2010)*; Redekopp and Ragusa (2013); Schmidt (2014)*; Swithenbank and DeNucci (2014); Thomas and Philpot (2012); Yelamarthi, Member, and Drake (2015)* |
| Flipped is more effective and/or no difference | Baepler, Walker, and Driessen (2014); Cavalli *et al.* (2014); Chetcuti, Hans, & Brent (2014); Choi (2013) |
| No difference | Buechler, Sealy, and Goomey (2014); Davies *et al.* (2013); Love, Hodge, Grandgenett, and Swift (2014); Mason, Shuman, and Cook (2013b); Olson (2014); Swift and Wilkins (2014); Talbert (2014); Velegol *et al.* (2015) |
| Flipped is less effective | Hagen and Fratta (2014); McClelland (2013) |
| Flipped is less effective and/or no difference | Lavelle, Stimpson, and Brill (2013) |

*Indicates statistical significance.

*Source: (Hashemifardnia et al., 2018)*

## 2.3.2 Motivations to Apply Flipped Learning in Higher Education

While the flipped learning became popular due to chemistry teachers Jon Bergmann and Aaron Sams implementing it in a high school class, it is particularly suitable for higher education settings. The maturity of learners at this stage is appropriate for self-learning, which is required in flipped learning for understanding the course content prior to class using video lectures and other resources rather than having in-depth discussions in-class on the topic and being able to conduct related activities. This provides learners with "opportunities to develop vital skills needed in the 21st century, including critical thinking, creativity, communications, and collaboration" (Aronson & Arfstrom, 2013). Flipped learning can also be conveniently used for large classes as students can use class-time effectively for discussion or class-activities with smaller groups formed amongst peers. Educators too are able to use their time in class for higher-level teaching and for guiding students. Moreover, it can be flexibly used for classes of all size as students have already studied the lecture on their own at a time of their convenience and can also ask questions at any time (Aronson & Arfstrom, 2013). Table-2.4 lists the top motivation for higher education educator to flip their courses.

**Table 2.4** Motivations for Educator to Flip Their Courses

Top Motivations for Higher Education Faculty to Flip their Courses

| Goal | Importance |
|---|---|
| Improve students' critical thinking/creative problem solving/higher-order thinking/21st century/professional skills | 1 |
| Increase student participation, engagement, and motivation | 2 |
| Improve students' team-based skills and peer-to-peer interaction | 3 |
| Customize/differentiate learning | 4 |
| Make students the center of learning/encourage student ownership of learning | 5 |
| Better faculty to student interaction | 6 |
| Increase faculty freedom/enjoyment | 6 |
| Improve learning outcomes | 6 |
| Dealing with absences | 7 |
| Encourage faculty collaboration | 7 |
| Compensate for limited classroom space | 7 |

Motivating factors were culled from 22 articles on Flipped Learning in a higher education setting.

*Source: (Aronson & Arfstrom, 2013)*

## 2.3.3 Challenges and Barriers Faced in Flipped Learning

Shnai (2017) conducted a systematic rigorous review of 49 articles selected out of a dataset of 1256 articles collected from Scopus, and focused his study on learners' and educators' feedback on reported gaps, drawbacks, and challenges. While flipped classroom can be advantageous in many ways, there are challenges for educators in designing and implementing it, and for students experiencing it for the first time. Educators face scarcity of resources and skills while preparing, developing and implementing the flipped classroom, and also issues related to the design and evaluation of innovative classrooms. In order to eliminate challenges faced by students, the educators focus on the learner' satisfaction, scores, engagement, personalization of time, and other measurements of learning with respect to the accessible resources (time, facilities, methods, skills). Both educator as well as learners specified the limited time as a major problem, while lack of resources was minor issue for students who mostly have basic equipment. The insights gained from issues in Shnai's study assisted author in suggesting guidelines and recommendations corresponding to each category of barriers faced by teachers and learners, as indicated in Table-2.5 (Shnai, 2017).

**Table 2.5** Barriers and Improvements

| Category of the barrier | Barriers | Most favorable solutions |
|---|---|---|
| | **Professors' barriers** | |
| Lack of Resources | Lack of time | Defining protected time for the course redesign. In addition, to Optimization of the time (McLaughlin, 2016). Preparation of some initial cost-effectiveness analysis to assess the future investments and payback (Shnai, 2016). For example, the increased time commitments for the first year of course redesign, can be covered by the next years (Ferreri, 2013) |
| Lack of Skills | Lack of skills | Workshops attendance<br>Meeting with colleagues to share experiences and evaluations (McLaughlin, 2016) |
| Design challenge | Low personalization.<br>Gaps in student understanding and free riders | Using a feedback system to gather opinions of each person in the class and estimate overall perception (Rodriguez, 2016) |
| | **Students' barriers** | |
| Design issues | Students unfamiliar with the flipped classroom concept (Gilboy, 2015) | Instructions supply for the students in advance (Gilboy, 2015; Kim,2014; Mason, 2013)<br>Check the understanding and confidence of students |

*Source: Shnai 2017*

## 2.5 Pedagogical Framework and Course Design for Flipped Learning

Educators have their own styles of teaching and they differ from one individual to other. There is inherent freedom for them to design the course delivery and to plan for it. With the academic freedom that educators demand, it is important that some guidelines or frameworks be in place where they can design and plan their course delivery. In the case of flipped learning, identifying the factors that may/may not contribute to its effectiveness is important to come up with such framework (Eppard & Rochdi, 2017). Based on broad heuristics for effective and efficient teaching and learning approaches and for the core principles of learning (Table-2.6), a pedagogical framework for the evidence-based flipped classroom was developed, as indicated in Figure 2.8 (Sale & Cheah, 2017).

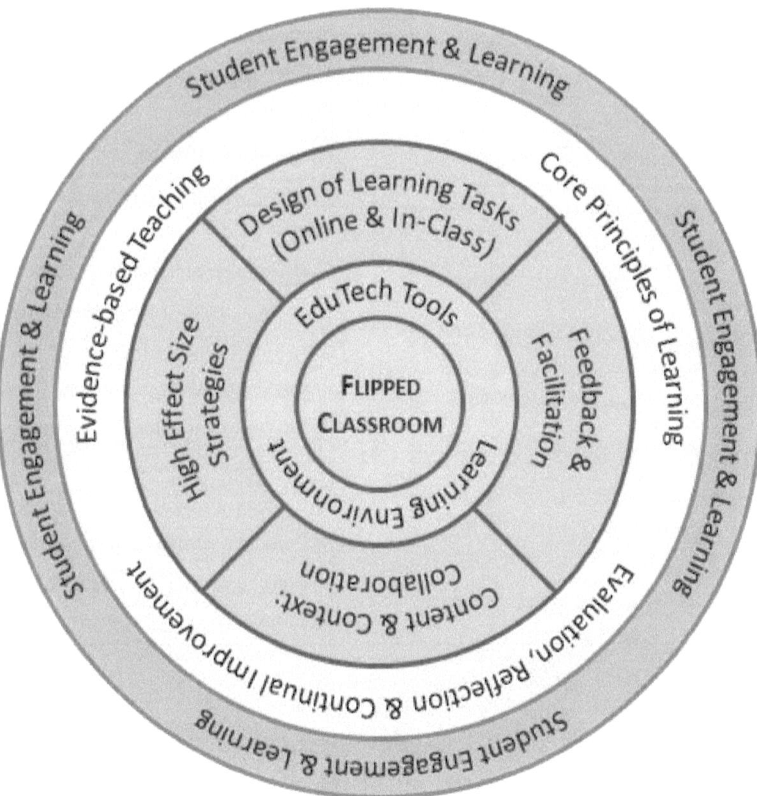


**Figure 2.8** Framework for Evidence-based Flipped Classroom

*Source: (Sale & Cheah, 2017)*

**Table 2.6** Heuristics and Core Principles of Learning

| Heuristics for effective and efficient teaching and learning approach | Core principles of learning |
|---|---|
| • Good learning design is *always* grounded on evidence-based practice, incorporating Core Principles of Learning<br>• Information-communication technologies are used *strategically* and *creatively* to enhance specific aspects of the learning process<br>• The completed blended learning design *maximizes* the affordances of a range of learning modes and mediums | • Motivational strategies are incorporated into the design of learning experiences<br>• Learning goals, objectives and proficiency expectations are clearly visible to learners<br>• Learners prior knowledge is activated and connected to new learning<br>• Content is organized around key concepts and principles that are fundamental to understanding the structure of a subject<br>• Good thinking promotes the building of understanding<br>• Instructional methods and presentation mediums engage the range of human of senses<br>• Learning design takes into account the working of memory systems<br>• The development of expertise requires deliberate practice<br>• A psychological climate is created which is both success-orientated and fun<br>• Assessment practices are integrated into the learning design to promote desired learning outcomes and provide quality feedback |

*Source: (Sale & Cheah, 2017)*

Sale and Cheah (2017) in developing a pedagogical framework for flipped learning, integrated all of the above features in addition to specifically combining schemes for high effect sizes as well as applying educational technology tools (EduTech tools) in order to enable student online learning both inside and outside of class, and to evaluate the effectiveness of flipped learning implementation from the educators' perspective as well as the students' perspective based on their feedback noted in the system (Sale & Cheah, 2017). A framework is shown in Figure-2.8, with the outermost ring being the primary aim of teaching, which is to engage students in their learning. The next ring depicts the application of the core principles of learning in the design of learning tasks, followed by ring that emphasizes out-of-class and in- class components using high effect size strategies, where peers (students) collaborate with each other and the learning process is supported by effective facilitation and timely feedback from the educator. Lastly, the inner circle is the learning environment and the use of EduTech tools as key factors for flipped classroom effectiveness. This framework is the most comprehensive attempt to date that addresses the exciting, multi-faceted nature of flipped classroom using an evidence-based approach.

For designing a flipped classroom, Sale and Cheah (2017) outline the key points as follows:

i. Learning objectives and the level of proficiency

ii. Learning outcomes as often detailed in the course outline

iii. Learning tasks that should not be overwhelming, but ones that stimulate students to devote time in going through them, requiring assimilation of motivational strategies

iv. Effective and creative use of EduTech tools such as Web 2.0

v. Instructional methods and presentation mediums should be engaging.

vi. A learning environment that promotes student participation, both outside the class when online and inside the class during activities. Sale (2015) offered a strategy based on SHAPE – stories, humor, activities, presentation style, and examples for creating desirable learning environment (Sale & Cheah, 2017).

vii. Build-up of students' prior knowledge for promoting collaborative learning among students that is also useful in facilitating their intellectual process

viii. Use of quality feedback with students as formative assessment

ix. A conducive learning environment that motivates students to take responsibility for monitoring their own learning

The recently published case study done by Tomas, Evans, Doyle, and Skamp (2019) explored how a flipped classroom supported students' engagement and learning. Based on the findings of this study, the authors proposed a "Flipped Learning Continuum". The case study was conducted using mixed-methods, including a student survey at the end of the semester and a narrative account of the educators' experience of enacting the active learning strategies in class. It was reported that all of the students believed that their high level engagement in the learning content prior to class through videos supported their learning, but their views/preferences differed for flipped versus traditional lectures (Tomas et al., 2019). It was also noted that the students on their own were unwilling to do the planned activities, especially those involving more challenging concepts, and educators had to spend a substantial amount of time in the beginning of the class to review key concepts. As a conclusion of this study, the authors have proposed a "Flipped Learning Continuum" that promotes different levels of student-centered learning and autonomy, depending on the students' learning needs and their readiness for a flipped learning approach. The same study also outlines students' as well as educators' perspectives about the flipped learning approach, as described below.

**Students' Perspectives** – The majority of the students responded positively to the flipped learning approach.

i. Videos – They provide students with the necessary knowledge that prepares them better for class activities. Additionally, the videos delivers learning content in concise but comprehensive manner, including visual representations through diagrams and illustrations and learning, thus providing in-depth knowledge for better understanding. The added advantage is the possibility to watch videos repeatedly as needed for better understanding and allowing for learning at the student's own pace.

ii. Flipped learning approach – Most students agreed that the flipped learning approach stimulates learning, with one-third of the students surveyed for this study neither agreeing nor disagreeing, or not believing in this approach.

iii. The opinion varied on the flipped learning approach in comparison to traditional lecture instruction being more engaging, with half of the respondents agreeing, and the rest being either neutral or not agreeing.

iv. Half of the students preferred the flipped classroom to the traditional classroom, with the other half either undecided or not preferring the flipped classroom over traditional classroom.

**Educators' perspectives** – The two educators, Louisa and Snowy, in this study narrated their experience in enacting the active learning strategies, whereby they had to adjust their planned activities because of elements that were not anticipated and somewhat unexpected in the beginning of running the course. Thus, the flipped learning model evolved with the following adjustments made:

i. Prior to the class – The flipped videos were supplemented with the online modules and readings for improved student engagement.

ii. At the start of the class – The flipped video content was revisited in class along with the educator providing further clarification if the students were unable to answer questions correctly.

iii. At the middle point of the class – Once the required understanding was reached, the educators guided and supported the students in progressing with the planned activities.

Various research scholars have made suggestions and noted observations to deal with effective and successful flipped classroom experience by adjusting strategies, such as:

i. Conveying clear expectations, encouraging students to be accountable for their self-learning outside of class time (O'Flaherty & Phillips, 2015)

ii. Conducting quizzes regularly with weightage assigned for evaluation in order to motivate students to complete required learning prior to class (Bishop & Verleger, 2013)

iii. Blended learning, where both educator-led and student-centered pedagogy approaches are used specially during the students' first year, which is an important phase of transition to higher education (Kift 2009)

iv. Resistance from first year students in taking responsibility for self-learning due to their expectancies and preconceived notions about the educator's role (Baird & Mitchell, 1987 cited in Karabulut-Ilgu, Jaramillo Cherrez, and Jahren 2018)

v. Unwillingness of students to participate in the online course components, particularly students, who chose to study on-campus with the expectation of having direct lecture delivery from proficient educators (Jefferies 2015 cited in (Bishop & Verleger, 2013), etc.

The strategies used by two educators Tomas and Evans (2019), in adjusting the needs of the students to modify flipped learning (Tomas et al., 2019), and the above suggestions/observations made by research scholars, seeded the idea of a "Flipped Learning Continuum," as shown in Figure 2.9. Here the learning ecosystem draws on aspect of both traditional approach and flipped approach, moving gradually from traditional lectures to a flipped classroom. This obviously depends on the students' ability to learn independently and their progress through their studies. Howitt and Pegrum (2015) made an interesting observation in this regard that postgraduate students "are often more motivated and committed than undergraduate students" (Howitt & Pegrum, 2015).

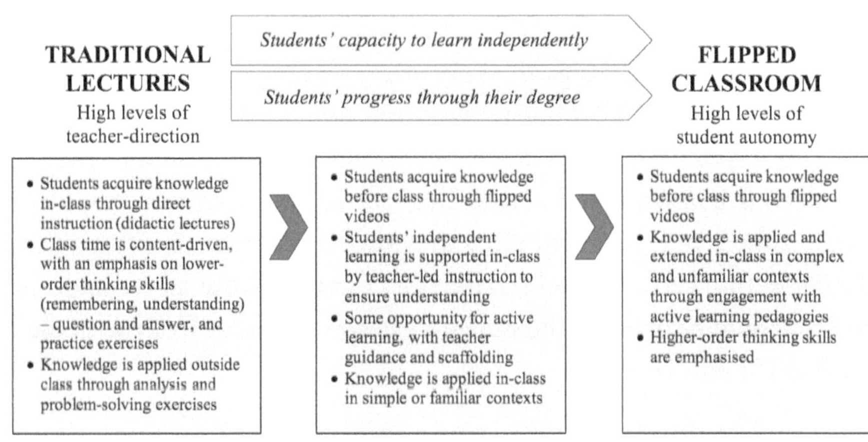


**Figure 2.9** Flipped Learning Continuum

*Source: (Tomas et al., 2019)*

Hao (2016) has also made a similar observation, that before plunging into flipped learning, students need to be introduced to the flipped learning concept gradually while providing them with support to develop specific attributes (such as self-directed learning skills) in order to increase their readiness for the student- centered nature of flipped classrooms (Hao, 2016). Maycock (2019) cautions about initiating flipped learning, for which the pedagogy design is based on the fundamental philosophy of active learning, thus requiring proper prior preparation and guidance to students, such as apprising them the need to make notes (just as they do in traditional lecture session). They felt that "perhaps, a flipped learning approach is better suited to students engaging in later stage modules at undergraduate level, after they have a competence in the specialist domain area" (Maycock, 2019). Related to this, Moravec and colleagues (2010) studied the result of a 'partial flip' where the in-class component also includes the lecture component, which led to a 21 percent improvement in student performance (Moravec et al., 2010). However, Bishop and Verleger (2013) argue that this denotes a "shortcoming" of the flipped classroom (Bishop & Verleger, 2013), while at the same time Tomas et al. (2019) counter argue for some teacher-led instruction, depending on the students' learning needs and their readiness for a flipped learning approach (Tomas et al., 2019).

According to Talbert (2014), the factors for the effective flipped classroom are: "(i) very organized pre-class assignments that are equipped towards presenting the students with the new theoretical notions, (ii) tools for responsibility to guarantee that students will finish the required pre-class assignments and out-of-class work, (iii) activities should be well planned and designed, attractive for the students to engage with during lecture time and (iv) the lines of correspondence all through the course should be open, so the students can communicate freely with their professor" (Talbert, 2014).

## 2.6 Factors Impacting the Adoption of the Flipped Classroom

The adoption of flipped learning depends to a large extent on the skills required on the part of both educators as well as learners, especially technological skills and building activities around that for learning. According to the International Society for Technology in Education (ISTE) 2016, the skills for learners are "empowered learner, digital citizen, knowledge constructor, innovative designer, computational thinker, creative communicator and global collaborator." The development of these skills obviously demands more active learning methodologies with different activities designed specifically for the classroom. Various approaches have transpired as a provision or an alternative to traditional classrooms that utilizes the technology appropriately, such as online learning, distance learning, blended learning, and flipped learning, which can provide students with a learning environment to develop their skills. All of these require increased workloads on part of educator, who has to prepare course videos for each topic, plan activities in accordance with the readiness of students, prepare class activities for deeper understanding and appreciation of the topic and system to regularly provide constructive feedback on and evaluation of the student's performance.

Educators' need to be conversant with ICT skills and software tools in order to integrate them for flipped classroom. In this respect, research scholars have found that aged educators are hesitant to incorporate technology (Vanderlinde, Aesaert, & Van Braak, 2014; Venkatesh, Morris, Davis, & Davis, 2003); male educators scored higher than female educators in their perceived use of ICT (Teo, 2014); and the key driving factor for the integration of ICT is associated with suitable learning activities (Hennessy, Ruthven, & Brindley, 2005). While this can be a challenging factor in the implementation of the flipped learning approach, the freely available software tools for creating lessons suitable for the flipped classroom model can be seen as a solution. There are a number of online platforms that offer wide range of features for creating lessons, including video resources, opportunity for adding text information explaining the lesson, tools for taking notes while watching lectures, and building in questions during the video or at the end demanding answers from students. This allows for the tracking of the learning progress and makes students active participants in their own learning process. Examples of such software tools and platforms are Moodle, EduCanon, Teachem, YouTube, VideoNotes, Bluebbr, Zaption, EdPuzzle, BlendSpaces, etc. The advantages of using these platforms for creating lessons for the flipped classroom range from being free and web-based; having user friendly interfaces with the drag & drop function; using different types of resources – text, pictures, videos, questions; sharing and embedding in web; tracking progress of assigned students with immediate feedback from them; reusing video tutorials created by other teachers in the platform; and interactivity – disruption of the video at a certain point in response to a question. However at the same time there are disadvantages as well, such as the inability for exporting, standards are not supported; some platforms require registration to be able to solve quizzes; and the inability to transfer the marks from these platforms to LMS (Angelova etal., 2014).

The main criticism of the flipped classroom approach is the lack of trained educators for this flipped learning approach. This would definitely require revision in the curricula of the education faculties, which includes information about the flipped classroom and training courses on this approach (Serin & Khabibullin, 2019).

## 2.7 Strategies for Successful Implementation of Flipped Learning

It is important to have some strategies in order to implement flipped learning successfully, as both educators and students do not have prior experience in it. "The flipped classroom requires numerous activities and the lack of adequate access to required technology by students make it uninteresting for lecturers to use. As the access to technology and data for internet browsing gets improved and easily available to support adequate learning and students' engagement, many lecturers would be willing and encouraged to implement the flipped classroom" (Cheng et al., 2019). Thus, adopting the following strategies could be useful for educators to implement flipped learning successfully:

i. Students should be well informed of their ability to access the videos to be used, which are generally in-house, especially if YouTube videos are prohibited for use by institute.

ii. Videos should be short and concise, covering the relevant material. If needed videos could be module-wise and released for viewing gradually.

iii. Video lectures from same person can be boring, thus variety should be encouraged instead of the videos being produced by one person. For this, educators can incorporate the vast assorted quantity of resources and materials available on Internet, especially since it requires time and technical skills, which all do not possess. There are many free online resources that could be used, such as khanacademy.com, Sophia.org, Moodle.org, etc.

iv. Diversity in activities, contents, and videos engages students more.

## 2.8 Flipped Learning Use in Higher Education in India – Current Status and Challenges

Not many Indian research scholars have published on flipped learning and very few publications could be found through a Google search on Internet. However, these published studies in general do indicate that the postgraduate students in India accept the idea of flipped classroom. The findings of one of the study done in India by Amula and Balakrishnan (2015) show that the mean was greater than 2.5 for all factors (for both experience and challenges), indicating the acceptance of flipped learning. For six of the factors related to experience, the mean score exceed 3.0, while for challenges mean score exceeded only for one factor. Furthermore, the cumulative mean scores for all of the factors for both experience and challenges were 2.90 and 2.74 respectively, higher in the case of experience. This indicates that the students in India are receptive to the idea of flipped learning. This differs to the findings of the research scholars cited in this study, "that the learning culture between the east and the west differs greatly" (Nisbett, 2003; Wang, 2006). The acceptance of the flipped classroom in India is similar to that in the West. The possible reason could be the closing of the digital gaps that existed between the countries, and global digital connectivity (Amutha & Balakrishnan, 2015).

India has around 1000 universities of higher education, and implementing the flipped learning pedagogical approach successfully can be a daunting task. Taking a cue from prime institutes in India, the Indian Institutes of Technology (IITs) in Delhi, Bombay, and Kharagpur, which have tried flipped learning, using it for some of their lectures, other technical education institutes in India have also begun to build up resources and a few of the educators there have begun to adopt a flipped learning pedagogy for their teaching. The Indian HRD Minister on 20 February 2019, launched the Operation Digital Blackboard, which technologically will make it possible for applying flipped learning pedagogy.

**Table 2.7** Experiences and Challenges – Flipped Classroom with Postgraduates in India

| ITEMS | MEAN | S.D. |
|---|---|---|
| **EXPERIENCE**<br>I like to learn in a flipped classroom | 2.61 | .722 |
| I learn better in a flipped classroom | 2.57 | .788 |
| I think differently in a flipped classroom | 3.00 | .674 |
| I use more resources in a flipped classroom | 3.30 | .635 |
| There is more communication in a flipped classroom | 2.91 | .793 |
| There is more discussion in a flipped classroom | 2.91 | .733 |
| I have an enriching learning experience in a flipped classroom | 2.87 | .626 |
| Flipped classroom helps me to develop problem solving skills | 2.91 | .668 |
| Flipped classroom provides an enjoying learning experience | 2.91 | .668 |
| Flipped classroom helps me to generate more new ideas | 3.04 | .825 |
| **CUMULATIVE MEAN FOR EXPERIENCE** | **2.90** | |
| **CHALLENGES** | | |
| I am adequately prepared to learn in a flipped classroom environment | 2.61 | .783 |
| I do not have any problems of learning in a flipped classroom | 2.48 | .511 |
| I can accept the flipped classroom concept of learning | 2.74 | .541 |
| I do not have enough time to learn in a flipped classroom | 2.87 | .815 |
| Learning in a flipped classroom is better than learning in the traditional lecture classroom | 3.13 | **4.170** |
| I have difficulties accessing materials/resources in the flipped classroom. | 2.30 | .765 |
| I do not have enough time to look for materials for flipped classroom | 2.78 | .671 |
| The in-class discussion is very productive for learning | 2.83 | .491 |
| Flipped classroom required me to do more work than traditional lecture classroom | 3.17 | .717 |
| I experience less problems in a flipped classroom | 2.48 | .730 |
| **CUMULATIVE MEAN FOR EXPERIENCE** | **2.74** | |
| **OVERALL MEAN SCORE FOR EXPERIENCE AND CHALLENGES** | **2.82** | |

*Source: (Amutha & Balakrishnan, 2015)*

The All India Council for Technical Education (AICTE), the regulatory body for technical education institutions, wants to adopt this method of teaching in order to make sure that students are able to utilize their time in problem-solving in classrooms and are able to learn better, thereby making them more industry ready. The AICTE was ready to introduce this model of teaching in colleges affiliated with it from the 2019-20 academic sessions. There are over 10,000 technical colleges in the country regulated by the AICTE. To begin with, the council plans to introduce flipped learning in engineering and management institutions. The colleges have been asked to adopt the flipped classroom model initially at the first-year level from the 2019-20 academic session. The council is in the process of uploading lecture videos and other study material on its website so that it can be made available to the teachers. It will also provide training to educators in colleges that want to adopt the model so that flipped learning can be implemented in a better manner.

Any new social experiments such as adaptive learning, gamification, and cooperative learning are welcomed by the education fraternity, but looking at the social realities, each new process of learning takes time to percolate down and to yield positive outcome for India. Flipped learning will need to be fine-tuned according to the Indian standards of diversity, education quality, and the standards of teachers. Unawareness of importance of digital learning in India and its integration with new- age technologies with material learning is a major challenge. However, with the infrastructure challenges in India, it needs to be seen whether it is practically possible to implement this concept. The main problem in India and other developing countries is the large digital divide, slow Internet penetration, and inept administration. Various digital schemes, such as SWAYAM and E-Paathshala are already in the offering, but no follow up audits or data driven reports have proven their efficacy.

Broadly, four challenges of flipped learning adoption and implementation in India can be summarized:

i. A lack of student discipline – For pupils, who have not had any exposure to flipped learning, the less conventional setup can be a challenge. Students can struggle with self-discipline and may turn up to class without having absorbed the lesson rendering the method pointless. Thus, an educator, when attempting to introduce the flipped classroom, should "start small," building student confidence with flipped tasks that in turn will help the teacher practice and prepare for the bigger change. This "soft" introduction gives pupils and teachers the chance to learn without becoming overwhelmed.

ii. Lack of teaching resources – Content is vital to creating a successful flipped classroom. However, a new approach often requires fresh resources. With spare time being the one thing that few teachers have in excess, the thought of designing and creating new content can be enough to turn even the most enthusiastic of teachers off. However, with many educators now creating and sharing resources online, teacher-authored content designed to support flipped learning could provide the answer.

iii. Old-fashioned classrooms – The layout of the traditional classroom is another obstacle to flipped learning. Collaboration, communication, and creativity are at the heart of this method, but fostering these skills is almost impossible with pupils inactive in rows of desks all day. Savvy teachers can however implement a more flexible classroom with the minimum amount of fuss, resources, and disruption – boosting student engagement and helping pupils to learn more effectively.

iv. Lack of equipment – Video conferencing technologies, screen-casting tools, and cloud-based platforms that let teachers create and deliver lessons all help to create the flipped classroom. However, poor quality, faulty, and out of date ICT equipment are some of the main reasons for teachers not using technology in the classroom and this can be a barrier to success. Likewise, flipped learning requires students to have access to the Internet and a computer or mobile device at home. However, this is not always the case, and it is important not to create a barrier for those students, who do not have the necessary technical gadgets or connections. To get around this, teachers have to put a back-up plan in place for all students, showing them what to do if the Internet goes down or if they do not have access to it. This could include identifying safe learning spaces with Wi-Fi, offering a borrowing library of computer devices, and providing learning content on USB drives.

## 2.9 Conceptual Framework of Flipped Learning in the Indian Context

The Figure 2.10 shows the conceptual framework for this study on flipped learning in the Indian context.

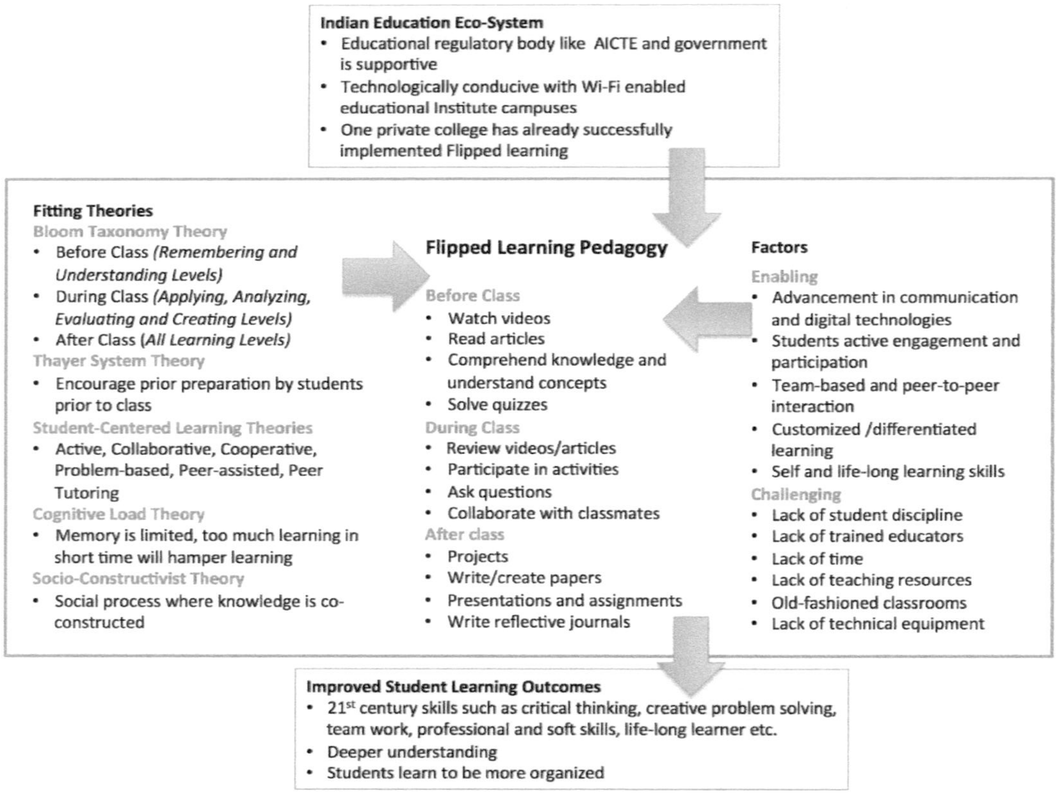

**Indian Education Eco-System**
- Educational regulatory body like AICTE and government is supportive
- Technologically conducive with Wi-Fi enabled educational Institute campuses
- One private college has already successfully implemented Flipped learning

**Fitting Theories**

Bloom Taxonomy Theory
- Before Class *(Remembering and Understanding Levels)*
- During Class *(Applying, Analyzing, Evaluating and Creating Levels)*
- After Class *(All Learning Levels)*

Thayer System Theory
- Encourage prior preparation by students prior to class

Student-Centered Learning Theories
- Active, Collaborative, Cooperative, Problem-based, Peer-assisted, Peer Tutoring

Cognitive Load Theory
- Memory is limited, too much learning in short time will hamper learning

Socio-Constructivist Theory
- Social process where knowledge is co-constructed

**Flipped Learning Pedagogy**

Before Class
- Watch videos
- Read articles
- Comprehend knowledge and understand concepts
- Solve quizzes

During Class
- Review videos/articles
- Participate in activities
- Ask questions
- Collaborate with classmates

After class
- Projects
- Write/create papers
- Presentations and assignments
- Write reflective journals

**Factors**

Enabling
- Advancement in communication and digital technologies
- Students active engagement and participation
- Team-based and peer-to-peer interaction
- Customized /differentiated learning
- Self and life-long learning skills

Challenging
- Lack of student discipline
- Lack of trained educators
- Lack of time
- Lack of teaching resources
- Old-fashioned classrooms
- Lack of technical equipment

**Improved Student Learning Outcomes**
- 21st century skills such as critical thinking, creative problem solving, team work, professional and soft skills, life-long learner etc.
- Deeper understanding
- Students learn to be more organized

**Figure 2.10** Conceptual Framework of Flipped Learning Pedagogy in the Indian Context

## Chapter 3

# RESEARCH METHODOLOGY

## 3.1 Research Design

The mixed-methods approach involving both qualitative as well as quantitative data was used to address the key research objectives. This method was adopted as it provides a better understanding of the research problems and questions compared to studies using single method, since it allows combining the weakness of one method with the strength of the other method (Creswell, 2014).

The research began with the understanding of the key concepts of flipped learning and the research that has been done until now on this topic through a literature review. This aided in identifying the research gaps and narrowing down the research objectives. For qualitative part, rapid appraisal methodology (RAM) was applied, and for quantitative data, an online questionnaire survey was conducted.

### 3.1.1 Study Area

The research study was conducted on flipped learning pedagogy for higher education in India; thus, the starting point was a case study conducted by visiting a college that has implemented flipped learning at the institute level for its undergraduate programs since 2016. This was followed by interviews with top administrators of some premium academic institutes, regulatory bodies, and related offices in India, and finally conducting focus group discussion with the educators of various higher education institutes across India in order to obtain an in-depth understanding of the issues related to the implementation of flipped learning. This in turn facilitated the development and collection of the primary data from the respondents (educators of higher education institutes across India) through and online questionnaire survey.

### 3.1.2 Data Sources

Primary data sources – The case study by visiting a college in India where researcher herself conducted interviews and made observations, interviews with top administrators and related offices' directors, and focus group discussions was the sources of the primary data collection. The online questionnaire survey was also used to further collect the primary data. Primary data are considered more reliable and researcher feels more confident about the data that is trustworthy, having been collected directly.

Secondary data sources – The available literature on flipped learning was the main source of secondary data used for the understanding of the benefits and applications of the flipped learning pedagogy. Books and journal papers, different articles, newspaper reports, websites, etc. were amongst the secondary data sources for this research study.

### 3.1.3 Rapid Appraisal Methodology

Rapid appraisal methodology was used for this study, as it is a "fast, cheap and valid" way to conduct research as professed by Rae Blumberg, a professor in the Sociology Department at the University of Virginia, and Professor Emerita of Sociology at the University of California, San Diego, who has vast experience in conducting research. The inherent flexibility in RAM makes it very useful for researchers. This is also called formative methodology, as during the course of conducting it, adjustments can be easily done on the topics of inquiry and can be continuously build upon. This is not possible when using a questionnaire survey. No matter how well the questions are designed and reviewed by peers, many times, it is observed that either some points are missed or not properly characterized. However, questionnaire can no longer be changed as it involves time and cost.

Using RAM is advantageous as it involves constant "triangulation" in order to cross-validate all findings. Triangulation means gathering data from at least two different sources – preferably using two different techniques (e.g. key informant interviews, focus groups, observation) – for each variable or issue being studied (Blumberg 2000). Prof. Blumberg suggests the following steps for RAM:

i. A literature review related to the topic from various sources such as journals, case studies, demographic data, and general reference documents and maps, and any project reports

   This was done beginning with a review of a book called "Flip Your Classroom" by Jonathan Bergmann and Aaron Sams, published in 2012, and several other books as referred to in Chapter 2 in the literature review. This was followed by reviewing selected research publications in the past decade in journals for further exploring the concept of the flipped learning, especially those focusing on higher education, with further narrowing down to its application and implementation in India for the higher education. Though there is not much literature available in India on this, the international research publications were reviewed, which was later applied and compared in the Indian context.

ii. Analysis of existing data related to the topic

   This was done particularly for this study as it was difficult to find existing data in the context of flipped learning being applied by educators in India (such as data on how many educators have adopted it), except the case of one college which has implemented flipped learning for its undergraduate programs across the institute since 2016 as mentioned earlier, which was known to the researcher while attending a workshop on flipped learning. Thus, it was taken up as case study and is explained in details under section 3.3.1. and for rest the information/data researcher had to rely on primary data sources.

iii. Interviews with key informants including gathering views of outsiders such as donors, NGOs, other institutions; and insider such as authorities/staff involved in the project and its management. This assisted in coming up with the first topic list to be used by present researcher.

The key informants considered as outsiders here were the persons in charge from the World Bank (not named for the sake of confidentiality as permission was not sought) involved in supporting the implementation of flipped learning in a college in India, concerned staff from the AICTE (All India Council of Technical Education), and the Director of the NPIU (National Project Implementation Unit), which is a special unit formed to undertake projects under the TEQIP (Technical Education Quality Improvement Program) – Phase I, II, and III which is in Phase III, wherein as part of this phase, 100 institutes have been selected for mentoring and training their educators in flipped learning. Further details on this are provided under section 3.3.2.

iv. Finally doing interviews with focus groups and key informants

Semi-structured interviews with key informants were held with several directors/vice chancellors/administrators of institutes. Further details on this are provided under section 3.3.2.

v. The need for researcher to be observant in the field while gathering information is also important in order to ensure that what is being reported match the researcher's intuitive expectations.

This was kept in mind while visiting the college as a case study and the E- learning Center to understand the intricacies involved in making video lectures.

vi. Focus group discussions should always begin with "icebreaker" questions to make the group comfortable and to open up the discussion in an informal manner. Focus group members should also be informed that there will be two types of questions with most questions to be responded by the whole group, but some questions were posted by the researcher to some individuals only. This was to ensure that the researcher had control of the group and that the discussions did not go awry. The findings from the focus group discussions should be verified back with the educators (participants).

All of the above-mentioned suggestions were adhered to during the preparation and while conducting the focus group discussion. The participants were invited for "high tea" to a restaurant with private room to have a discussion without any disturbance and as courtesy towards the participants for spending their valuable time with the researcher. The participants were informed that it would take an hour for the discussion; however, the participants were so keenly interested in the topic that it continued for more than two hours with further informal discussions continuing beyond that time. At the end, the researcher was asked to summarize and report back her understanding to the participants so that it could be verified and corrected immediately. More details on how the focus group discussion was conducted are provided under section 3.3.3.

### 3.1.4 Questionnaire Survey

The online questionnaire survey was developed after the comprehensive understanding was gained through the literature review, the college visit, and the interviews and the focus group discussion as described in section 3.1.3 in the procedures followed for the RAM. Additionally, a special report entitled "Faculty Focus – Flipped Classroom Trends: A Survey of College Faculty" was reviewed to be used as a basis for listing questions that encompassed various features of flipped learning, especially from the perspective of the educator's point of view (Faculty Focus, 2015).

It is well-known fact that garnering responses from self-administered questionnaire surveys is difficult as individuals find it time consuming. Thus, following the focus group discussion, the experiences and perceptions of educators about flipped learning, and suggestions or ideas that percolated out of discussions, were used in constructing statements that could be possible answers for the questions. These were then used for multiple choice questions so that the respondents could "click" without spending much time on answering, and with the option of "others" to leave it open for them to answer outside the multiple choice option as well. Further, since during the focus group discussion it was clear that though some kind of awareness was present about flipped learning, there was a lack of complete understanding; it was often confused with blended learning. Thus, after the first section on questions related to mainly information about the individuals, and questions about their understanding of flipped learning by clicking one of the options provided for the definition of flipped learning, the respondents were requested to go through the next section on the "Overview of the flipped learning" before moving to a further section on answering questions on their experience with and perception of teaching flipped learning. It was ensured that the time consumed to fill out the questionnaire survey was not more than 10-15 minutes as a safeguard to garner as much responses as possible. More details on the questionnaire survey are covered under section 3.3.4.

## 3.2 Unit of Analysis

The unit of analysis for this study was at three levels. For the case study, it is the college as a whole, including administrators, educators, and students. For the interviews, both outsider and insider key informants, i.e. persons in charge from the World Bank and AICTE, the Director of NPIU, directors/vice chancellors/administrators of the institutes, and individual educators were interviewed. For the focus group discussion also it was individual educators, with respondents for the questionnaire survey being individual educators as well.

## 3.3 Data Collection and Tools

With this research being done using a mixed methodology, each tool required a different methodology and use of appropriate strategy and tools. The sections below describes each one of them, and findings and data analyses is reported in Chapter 4.

### 3.3.1 Case Study of JIS College of Engineering, Kalyani, India

According to per Robert K. Yin, the case study research method is "an empirical inquiry that investigates a contemporary phenomenon within its real-life context." Furthermore, "[c]ase study research excels at bringing us to an understanding of a complex issue or object and can extend experience or add strength to what is already known through previous research." In order to understand the challenges and issues faced in the adoption and implementation of the flipped learning approach for the entire curriculum of its engineering college, a field visit was made to only one college that considers itself pioneer in this area in India.

In order to obtain complete information on the implementation process and challenges faced in the implementation and adoption of flipped learning pedagogy, it was important that the visit be made formally after seeking permission from top-level administration. This was envisaged to be useful in attaining access in order to interview the principal of the college, educators, and to intermingle with students in an informal way, and also to receive support in visiting their facilities and if possible attending a class in session. A formal letter was written to the chairman of the educational group to which the college belongs, certifying that the research study being conducted was for a doctoral study purpose and that the researcher was working at an academic institute in Thailand, with a request to allow the visit and to extend support. The researcher requested the president of the academic institute where she works to increase the chances of the request of the visit being entertained by the college administrators. This worked well and they not only allowed the visit but extended an invitation to visit during the time when an international conference was conducted, and as part of it, the students' paper presentations were also scheduled, and this allowed the researcher to observe and evaluate the students' performance and the impact that flipped learning had on them. With the help of the principle of the college, in addition to the interview with him, an interview was scheduled with the vice president for academic administration, and a dean and educator were assigned to let the researcher see the facilities of the college that supports the flipped learning ecosystem, including the specific classroom furniture layout, the video recording room, smart studios, etc.

The visit, with all the support provided by the college, helped to better understand the students' and educators' flipped learning experiences; interpretations of their learning and teaching skills growth, learning and strategies; challenges and barriers in implementation, execution, application; and strengths and needs as flipped learners or educators. First-hand experience by interacting with the students and educators directly and interviewing them provided insights into the execution of the class material, curriculum, time, and other resources from the students' perception.

### 3.3.2 Interviews with Key Informants

As part of gaining further insights into the adoption of flipped learning regarding the teaching and learning methods, the interviews were conducted with the top academic administrators and key persons involved in this area in order to understand the Indian education ecosystem with regards to flipped learning pedagogy use and awareness. The discussion during the interviews centered around the broad questions listed below, which were based on the concept of the flipped learning approach, perceived challenges in its use, and possible solutions or alternatives available. Since this research used a mixed research methodology, the intention behind the interviews was not to conduct any content analysis, but rather to understand the Indian education ecosystem suitability for flipped learning pedagogy.

i. What are educators' thoughts about flipped learning pedagogy?

ii. If educators have not implemented it, what are the reasons, such as challenges or issues that stop them from using it?

iii. Should it be left up to the choice of the individual educator to teach using flipped teaching, or should it be made mandatory or not allow it at all?

iv. Are facilities such as the flipped classroom, smart boards, smart studios, etc., available?

v. Do the educators have incentive to use flipped learning approach?

Prior to beginning the interviews, permission was sought to be able to disclose the individual's or his or her institute's/organization's name in the report, and also if audio recording could be used. None of the interviewees allowed using the individual's or institute's name; thus they were not mentioned specifically in this research study. However, interviewees were open to answering any questions with note taking allowed (instead of audio recording), making them able to answer the questions more informally and comfortably. As a researcher, who is experienced in coordinating such meetings, it was not an issue to take notes during the discussions. The researcher made report from the notes within a day or two after interview as it helped in recalling any points missed in making notes. Additionally, after the interview, the discussions were summed up and reconfirmed with the interviewee in order to ensure that the understanding was correct and that the concluding summary matched the was as per interviewees' discourse.

### 3.3.3 Focus Group Discussion

It has been suggested by Prof. Ray Blumberg to keep the following key points in mind while preparing for and conducting a focus group:

i. Number – The ideal number of participants is considered to be five, which could go up to a maximum ten. If number is larger, then there is fear of someone beginning to dominate the group and some members would become quite and not participate in the discussions or would be swayed by the dominant member's ideas.

ii. Homogeneity – The homogeneity of a group related to the topic to be discussed is important, with members coming from the same background, professions, and in some cases the same age group, etc. Furthermore, the moderator needs to ensure that no one has an edge over others in the group due to their position.

iii. Not for – A focus group discussion is not for having discussions of an intimate nature.

iv. No spy – Make sure that the focus group members are confident that the discussions are not leaked out of the group and that they are kept confidential.

The focus group discussion was intended to explore further the implementation/adoption of flipped learning/teaching in India. The group consisted of seven educators as participants from various institutions/universities covering different regions (northern, eastern, western, southern, and central) in India as indicated in the map in Figure 3.1. The list of participants for which the permission was sought to let the individual's and their institutes' names be noted, is provided in Table 3.1 below. The researcher herself was the moderator of the focus group discussion. Though a set of questions was prepared for the moderator to guide the discussion, flexibility to let the discussion flow organically rather than controlling was observed in order to allow for the free flow of ideas and dialogues. However, it was made sure that all of the questions were covered and none was left unattended to or unaddressed.

**Figure 3.1** Focus Group Discussion Participants

**Table 3.1** List of Participants in the Focus Group Discussion

| | | |
|---|---|---|
| 1 | Dr. Shiv Kumar Gupta<br>*Associate Professor* | *Indian Institute of Technology (IIT), Roorkee, Uttrakhand, India* |
| 2 | Dr. Sujit Gajananrao Metre<br>*Professor* | *Dr. Ambedkar Institute of Management Studies & Research, Nagpur, Maharashtra, India* |
| 3 | Dr. Nagarujana Nallam<br>*Assistant Professor* | *Indian Institute of Technology (IIT), Guwahati, Assam, India* |

| | | |
|---|---|---|
| 4 | Dr. T Kishore Kumar<br>*Professor* | *National Institute of Technology, Warangal, India* |
| 5 | Dr. Sarat Kumar Kotamraju<br>*Professor* | *K.L. University, Guntur, Andhra Pradesh, India* |
| 6 | Dr. Neeraj Pandey<br>*Associate Professor* | *National Institute of Industrial Engineering, Mumbai, Maharashtra, India* |
| 7 | Dr. Jagdish Singh<br>*Professor* | *Maulana Azad National Institute of Technology, Bhopal, Madhya Pradesh, India* |

**The following questions were prepared to lead the focus group discussion:**

i. Do you think that instead of traditional way of teaching, this type of active learning is more beneficial for students in India?

ii. So basically, all agree that it is beneficial. Will you flip if you are trained to do so and are provided with assistance regarding the technical aspects?

iii. What are the issues or challenges that stop educator from using this teaching method?

iv. What kind of support would you need if you want to use this teaching method at the institute level?

v. Should this teaching method be used across the institute level, or for some selected courses at the beginning stage? Are we ready to use it at the institute level?

vi. Should we slowly adopt it across the institute once we are ready within some time frame.

vii. What do you think is needed to support it at the government? What kind of policy framework should be there be?

viii. Is there a relevant question I missed? Anything else you want to tell me?

### 3.3.4 Questionnaire Survey, Sample Size, and Reliability

The aim of the survey was to carry out an analysis of the educators' experience/perception of flipped learning in the context of higher education in India, and to comprehend the knowledge, motivations, and needs that educators have to apply this model. The mixed-methods approach was used since quantitative data allows for conclusions that can be generalized, unlike qualitative data, which provides contextual information. Qualitative evaluations make a good complement, allowing one to do the following: study the underlying reasons for the obtained data in the quantitative surveys; understand some of their results; study in depth the dimensions, and even identify some others not identified yet but that worry the respondents; and finally, provide decisive information from the perspective of the participants. The instrument used in the study was an online questionnaire that included multiple choice questions on a Likert-scale (scale of 1-5) and open-ended questions to collect both the quantitative and qualitative data.

Using the knowledge gained through the case study and interviews, the online questionnaire survey was developed and another professor cum researcher verified the suitability of the items. The reliability of the instrument was established according to the responses provided by 20 another educators (academicians) and the questionnaire was then revised accordingly, incorporating the comments/suggestions made. This exercise proved useful, as based on the responses received and noting that the answers were repetitive, some of the questions were converted into multiple-choice questions that consumed less time in responding to.

Additionally, based on the suggestion of a professor during the validation process, all of the Likert-scale questions were made consistent with the 1-5 scale (prior to validation, one of the Likert question had a 1-4 scale). Further, the researcher; thus, they were merged into one question. The revised questionnaire was again circulated amongst these same 20 educators from different universities in India, and the resulting Cronbach alpha reliability index obtained was far above 0.6 required. This was circulated to the participants with a cover letter explaining the purpose of the research study and requesting educators to fill it out, as it was related to their own esteemed profession of teaching, and the study may result in an enhanced educational ecosystem in India with their valuable feedback in the form of responses to the questionnaire.

The online questionnaire survey (enclosed as Annex-1) was prepared using Google Form, which can be conveniently filled out even using smartphone. It was circulated through email and WhatsApp using snowball random sampling. Fifty educator members known to the researcher and that belonged to different category of institutes/ universities across India were sent email with cover letter and link to the online questionnaire survey. They were requested to forward it to their colleagues in their own institute, as well to the institutes where they know an educator or educators so that their colleagues could become aware of it.

The questionnaire was divided into four sections, with first section being simple information related to the respondents. The second section was to give overview of flipped learning for those that were not aware of this pedagogical approach, as well as for ensuring that the understanding of flipped learning was in the context of this research study. The third and fourth section had questions grouped together on different topics, with either multiple-choice options or questions on a Likert-scale.

The follow-up emails and WhatsApp messages (which is becoming a more convenient one-to-one informal communication) were sent frequently, and also giving feedback was provided on how many of their institute's colleagues had responded in order to obtain as many responses as possible. Weekly emails were sent, thanking the faculty members, who had responded with a request to further forward the questionnaire to their colleagues. As researcher, I was aware that collecting enough responses would be a challenge, especially from faculty members, who were busy and may not have been keen on filling out a questionnaire survey. However, constant reminders and personal emails and messages helped in finally obtaining a total of 306 responses within a period of two months between December 2019 and January 2020, out of which 9 entries were removed, with 1 being anonymous, 1 from a high school (not higher education institute), and 7 duplicate entries, thus leaving a total of 297 responses from more than 100 unique colleges and universities across India, i.e. approximately 10 percent of the higher education institutes in India, which included leading higher education institutions such as Indian institutes of technology, and various categories (Private, Public, State, Deemed, and Universities of National Importance) of universities, institutes, and colleges. It is believed that more responses could have been collected, as some of those that are not aware of or that did not have experience with flipped learning were reluctant to fill out the questionnaire. This was obvious from several emails received when reminders were sent to them, where they stated that they were too inexperienced in the field to answer. Due to time constraints, as per the Yamala sample calculation a sample size of 385 for a 95 percent confidence level with a 5 percent margin of error could not be reached. However, a sample size of 297 is far greater than 269, which was needed for a 90 percent confidence level with a 5 percent margin error. The questions were based on existing literature on flipped learning and previous studies that have been done on the topic, albeit outside the Indian context.

After the questionnaire survey was closed to input, a post Cronbach alpha reliability index was obtained, which resulted in more than a 0.758 or above value for all of the questions, and with average Cronbach value of 0.868 for all questions. The reliability test with corresponding values for each question is given in Table 3.2.

**Table 3.2** Cronbach's Alpha Reliability

| | | Cronbach's Alpha |
|---|---|---|
| 1. | Students are more engaged in a flipped course | .884 |
| 2. | Students' grades are improved in a flipped course | .884 |
| 3. | Students are not resistant to a flipped course | .888 |
| 4. | Students prefer a flipped course to the traditional approach | .885 |
| 5. | Students adapt to the flipped learning approach | .884 |
| 6. | Students ask more questions in a flipped course | .883 |
| 7. | Students come to class prepared for a flipped course | .884 |
| 8. | Students are more collaborative in a flipped course | .883 |
| 9. | Students see the value with a flipped learning experience | .882 |
| 10. | Students are comfortable using technology for a flipped course | .883 |
| 11. | Students build relationships/community feeling in a flipped course | .883 |
| 12. | Flipped teaching is implementable being more beneficial for students | .887 |
| 13. | Flippedteaching can be implemented across institute/university programs | .888 |
| 14. | Flipped teaching can be applied for selected courses only | .891 |
| 15. | Flipped teaching can be implemented incrementally for all programs across the institute/university | .892 |
| 16. | The experience of teaching a flipped course is positive | .893 |
| 17. | Teaching a flipped course is convenient | .896 |
| 18. | Preparing for a flipped course is convenient | .900 |

| | | |
|---|---|---|
| 19. | A flipped course covers more course content | .894 |
| 20. | Flipped teaching is more interactive | .892 |
| 21. | Workshops/trainings are conducted to encourage offering flipped learning | .896 |
| 22. | Technical support is provided to encourage offering flipped learning | .896 |
| 23. | Manpower support is provided to encourage offering flipped learning | .895 |
| 24. | Monetary incentive or promotion provided to encourage offering flipped learning | .895 |
| 25. | Teaching loads are reduced to allow preparing for flipped learning | .894 |
| 26. | Challenging with competing department goals | .758 |
| 27. | Not valued by colleagues/administrations | .758 |
| 28. | Not understood by colleagues/administration | .758 |
| 29. | Requires creativity/developing new strategies and ideas | .756 |
| 30. | Student resistance/lack of motivation | .760 |

Chapter 4

# FINDINGS AND ANALYSIS

This chapter describes the findings from the data collected and their analysis in order to address the research objectives of this study.

## 4.1 Application of Flipped Learning Pedagogy in Higher Education in India

### 4.1.1 Findings and Observations from a Visit to a College in India

In order to find out the real challenges and solutions in implementing flipped learning pedagogy in India, a case study was conducted by making a visit to the JIS College of Engineering (JISCE), in Kalyani, Kolkata, India; which was the first Institution in India to fully adopt flipped teaching in their undergraduate engineering program. JISCE belong to the JIS group, which has many educational institutes in the field of engineering, arts, and sciences.

During the visit, the institute arranged inspection of the facilities, and interaction with the student, educators, and administrators. They have excellent facilities for conducting flipped classes and have made a large investment in the studio and classroom facilities. They began flipped classes three years prior to the writing of the present study, and the current batch is in its 3rd year, with first batch of students graduating in 2020. While interacting with the current students, very interesting insights were gained. The students said that when they first began to study using the flip mode, they were not very happy and it was completely new and difficult for them. However, as they got more acquainted with this pedagogy, they began to understand this new system and to like it, as this gave them lot of freedom to learn at their own pace and to better learning through interaction in the class. The facilitation and support from the professors were very important in this mode of learning. Since, it was new for the educator also, both students and the educators began with the flipped mode of learning and teaching in an exploratory mode using all resources available.

Initially the students did not like to do lot of work outside the class on their own and missed some classes, despite the fact that they were told that the classes were very important as their evaluation would be based on the class work and no final exams would be conducted. In the first year, during the mid-term, many students got an "F" grade as a result. Due to this, there was lot of agitation from the students, which escalated so much that one day, the principle of JIS College had to be confined to his office because of the agitated students. A lot of negotiation took place between the students and the administration of the college, and finally a compromise was reached – the midterm grades were waived in terms of being counted in the final grade, but the students had to attend the classes regularly.

The parents too were initially against this mode of teaching and questioned that if there was no midterm or final written exam, how could they be ensured that their children were performing in their studies? After many meetings held with the parents to educate them about the benefits of flipped learning, as it involves continuous evaluation of the students and their progress can be reviewed continually, they agreed to watch it for one or two semesters, and eventually, once they saw the benefits and improvement in the students, they began to applaud this system and complemented the administration and educator for their efforts.

There was another hurdle to overcome in terms of the university regulation regarding final and mid-semester exams, as there was no policy to exempt the students from these exams. The college approached the university management to waive off the aforesaid exams for the students studying using flipped learning pedagogy. After herculean efforts by the vice chancellor (VC) and senior administrators, the university senate allowed this exemption. The VC in an interview mentioned that the educator does not want to change or adopt a new system as it needs lot of effort, but he thought that it was very much the hour of need, and while educator recruitments were conducted it was ensured that only the educator that was open to adopting flipped learning pedagogy would get appointed.

The interaction with students in $2^{nd}$ and $3^{rd}$ year revealed that they had a very positive experience with flipped learning, and said that they understood the concepts very well and that it was more fun to do various activities together in class. The students helped each other to understand the subject better, and many students that were shy in the beginning slowly developed good communication skills and became more confident. They also mentioned that when they went to conferences and seminars, they found it much easier to present and interact on various topics compared to students from other institutions, who were taught in a traditional way.

The principal joined the institution in 2016 and he came from a university in Australia, where flipped pedagogy was a common mode of teaching. He elaborated on the challenges he faced in implementing flipped learning in the college. First, he had to convince the management to adopt this methodology for the engineering students with its obvious benefits for the students and learning outcomes. He was also convinced that this would be a unique proposition for the college to achieve a higher ranking and to attract the best students to obtain admission to the college. Once the management was convinced and permitted him to go ahead with flipped teaching, the real challenge was to convince and get permission from AICTE (regulatory body for technical education in India) and the university to which the college was affiliated.

The principal approached AICTE in order to obtain the necessary permission to waive-off the final examinations' regulation. During this course, he also approached the World Bank, and they proved to be very helpful in convincing the regulators with their global perspective and experience. The World Bank also agreed to fund some pilot projects for flipped learning. It was suggested that the key interviewees for this research study should include the concerned staff from AICTE, and the director of NPIU. The role and support of the director of NPIU (National Project Implementation Unit), a special unit formed to undertake projects under the TEQIP –Phase I, II, and III – was very important for the success of this initiative. The TEQIP, Phase III, is now under progress, where 100 institutes have been selected for mentoring and training their educators in flipped learning. JIS College has received a pilot project to train several batches of educators on flipped learning, which began in November 2019 on their college campus.

The principal further informed that the educators teaching in JIS had to be trained in flipped learning pedagogy and over the time they would also have to improve the use of this pedagogy. They collaborated with MEF University in Turkey, which is also one of the pioneers in flipped learning implementation for their whole university. They invited professors from MEF University and had JIS educators trained in flipped teaching. The educator role is very important, and he/she should be alert in class while group discussions are taking place. He/she should facilitate and supervise them. At the end, he/she summarizes the topic based on the students' discussions and adds any missing elements. At times, the educators themselves also learn new things from the students.

Another challenge was to create an appropriate infrastructure for flipped learning with new classrooms, multi-media studios and smart boards, high speed Internet, and other facilities. The students, educators, and the whole campus were to be digitally enabled. The places of learning were also designed differently where the facilitator is in the middle of the class, while the learners are seated in clusters of their choice from vantage angles as it is the prerequisite of the adult learning at tertiary level. The utmost care was taken to create the convenient ergonomic conditions for the progression of learning, especially; using the flip learning technique. However, the smaller clusters had been given to each student for a greater chance to participate equally and accordingly the learning could be evaluated more objectively.

The pictures in Figures 4.1, 4.2 in Findings and Analysis on page number 79 and 80, namely; 4.3 and 4.4 have depicted various facets apropos the flip learning from tete-a-tete with the expert, the subsequent settings required and the moments of wit; mirth and happiness enabled by flip learning.

**Figure 4.1** Krishna Nath Pandey with Facilitator

**Figure 4.2** The Beginning of the Process

**Figure 4.3** Autonoetic mode of Flip Learning

**Figure 4.4** Interaction and Valediction

During the visit, incidentally, the college had organized an international conference, and the educators and students were participating in the conference. There were three parallel sessions in which the students were presenting their research papers jointly authored with educators on different topics. External experts were invited to listen to their presentations and to evaluate them. I attended one of the sessions where 15 students presented papers. After the presentation, each presenter was asked tough questions and it was a pleasant surprise to see that they could answer well with full understanding of the concepts. It was not just the presentation and communication skills that were good, but that the students had full knowledge of the concepts was remarkable.

During the discussion with the vice president for institution development, she mentioned that the introduction of flipped learning has been very beneficial for the college as the student intake has increased and the intake quality also went up. They received very encouraging reports from the industries where the students took up internships and various inter-college conferences and events that the students of JIS College attended.

With this case study, it was quite clear that the adoption of flipped learning is indeed challenging, as most of the ecosystem for higher education is still occupied by a traditional mindset and they want to continue with traditional teaching methods. However, once they become aware of new teaching methods, such as flipped learning, they adopt them very quickly and achieve better learning outcomes. They also become a catalyst to spread these new pedagogies in higher education. The underlying requirement for successful implementation is the commitment of the management and the consistent effort of the administration and educator to ensure a supportive ecosystem. The information on the flipped learning technological infrastructure requirements, teams, format for evaluating the students, and guidelines, etc. used by JIS College can be found in Appendix F.

### 4.1.2 Findings from the Interviews

The following interviews were conducted in person and the findings are summarized as below:

i. Director of the Indian Institute of Technology (IIT) in India

   The first interview was held with the director of one of the Indian Institutes of Technology (IIT), which falls under the category of an Institute of National Importance. As of the time of this writing, there were 23 IITs in India and the total number of seats for undergraduate programs run in these IITs was 11,279. Every IIT is linked to the others through the IIT Council, which oversees their administration. The director was well aware of flipped learning pedagogy, but said that they were not doing it currently. However, he understood very well that this would be the future of teaching, and so they have begun to take steps toward it by first implementing blended learning, and asking educators to have 20 percent teaching using blended learning. They also have established a full-fledged e-learning center and he suggested that I interview the coordinator of the e-learning center to get more details on how they were working, which eventually would help them move toward flipped learning. He was of the opinion that the institutes should not make a fast leap to this mode of teaching until the ecosystem is fully developed for doing so, until their classrooms have all of the necessary facilities, until the campus is fully Wi-Fi enabled with high Internet speed required to download videos and lessons from anywhere, until the teachers are well trained in using this teaching method, and so on. He believed in a step-wise move toward this goal to see what adjustments would be needed. The training and motivation of the educator are crucial for the success of this mode of learning/teaching. The support at the policy level from the government is also important and he expected this in the new education policy.

ii. Coordinator, E-Learning Center at an IIT, India

The coordinator of the e-learning center explained how they are utilizing this center and providing educator members with the necessary support in creating digital video lectures. Incentive is provided to each educator by giving him or her 100,000 Rupees (approx. 1,500 USD) per subject course + 50,000 Rupees (750 USD) for each re-run of the subject course. Even then, many educators do not participate in it, with the trend being more participation from younger educators. The concern is that they may not be needed later to run courses with recorded lessons being used, plagiarism issues, etc. However, there are also incentives for educators to revise the courses in 3- 4 years, in which case they would again receive 50,000 Rupees. The other incentive was that these video lectures go to the national MOOCs platform "Svayam" provided by MHRD. Any student is free to use it, and if he or she also completes the course and sits for the in-center exam, he/she gets a certificate from IIT. Additionally, each student is allowed to take any two such MOOCs from the selected list of courses for each program.

iii. Vice Chancellor, University of Science and Technology

The vice chancellor (VC) had some basic ideas about the concept, but like many educators and academicians, he thought that it was just producing video lectures and online resources for blended learning. However, he had keen interest to know about what flipped learning entailed. He asked me to brief him about my visit and my first-hand experience with this learning pedagogy at the College of Engineering, which I visited as part of the case study. The interview became more of a discussion on flipped learning rather than questioning him about it, with clarification made on the difference between blended and flipped learning. He wondered and wanted to know if this helped in developing only the soft skills of the students or if they also would become clearer about basic concepts and be more knowledgeable. My observations from the JIS College of Engineering students' presentations and answering questions on topics were briefed to him. To my surprise he told me that he was keen to learn from me, being a researcher on this topic, since they are actually one of the institutes selected to train their educators in flipped learning by the NPIU under TEQIP-III. He was convinced that this training would be beneficial for his institute's educators. He then toured me around his institute's facilities and infrastructure that he was developing so that this mode of teaching could be used. He also arranged an interview with another vice chancellor of the university whom I interviewed the next day, as discussed below.

iv. Vice Chancellor, Skill University

The vice chancellor has around 30 years of corporate experience with companies such as IBM, Schneider, etc. He is well aware of the need of industries with staff with required skills and of academic quality. He informed me that though the university was established 2 years before the interview, the first intake would be in August of the following year because developing an appropriate curriculum is in line with industry needs. The educators were recruited 2 years after the university was established, but instead of asking them to teach right away, they were asked to work at selected industries and develop their curriculum in line with the skills required by the students' prospective employees. The curriculum would have full-fledged internship elements included for the students. The model is very interesting, and he was also convinced that if classroom teaching adopted active learning such as flipped learning, it would certainly be successful.

v. Director, National Project Implementation Unit

The director of the NPIU is responsible for the implementation of the TEQIP under the Ministry of Human Resources (MHRD). He explained how they have progressed from the TEQIP-I, II, and

III projects, which are all successful according to the outcomes and appropriate utilization of funding provided by the World Bank. He informed me that even though he believes that flipped learning pedagogy is beneficial for students, he was initially apprehensive if India had the resources to train such a large number of educators for this pedagogy. On the World Bank's advice, he visited the JIS College of Engineering in Kalyani to have first-hand experience, and his views were similar to the present author's observations (noted under section 4.1.1.). He informed that they have selected JIS for a pilot project to train several batches of educators and later on will decide about further training according to the outcomes. Under TEQIP-III, around 100 institutes have been selected for mentoring and training in it. Mostly they are from the states that are lagging behind developed educational institutes. The top-ranking institutes such as IITs, NITs, etc. have well established systems and they can follow on their own later using the guidelines that will be established based on this project.

### 4.1.3 Findings from the Focus Group Discussion

For outlining the key drivers for the adoption of flipped learning by educators in India, focus group discussions were conducted with seven educators from different institutes that fall under different categories, such as deemed university, private universities, institutes of national importance, etc. This helped in identifying the key drivers and challenges based on their experiences/perceptions of flipped learning and its implementation in India, which further helped to develop the questionnaire survey.

During the focus group discussion, it became clear that all of the participants have some ideas about the flipped learning concept; however, only 3 out of 7 members had a clear understanding of the concept. Initially some members argued that they actually do this kind of active learning in their laboratory classes and tutorials and that there is nothing new in this concept. However, once the concept was explained in greater details and the benefits it has, most agreed that they were open to transitioning into teaching using the flipped learning approach.

All of the participants felt that the current education ecosystem and infrastructure were not suitable for this teaching mode, and it should be done slowly in steps. Many opined that it may not be suitable for all subject areas and courses. There was a difference of opinion as to whether first it should be initiated by the 20 percent top ranked universities of India, or by the rest of the lower ranked 80 percent of universities. The argument in favor for the top universities to adopt this approach first was that they have all the required resources and systems in place, thus making it easier for them to adopt it. Moreover, the low ranked universities look up to them, and generally follow their pattern, so they can follow later. The counter argument to implementing it first for the rest of the 80 percent of lower ranking universities was that educators there are more adaptable and flexible in their approach. Moreover, to market themselves and compete and come up to the level of the top universities, they are eager to adopt new things, while the top ranking educators are a bit rigid and like to maintain the status quo. In general, however the consensus was towards 80 percent of the universities adopting it first, as they would be more flexible in doing so and with the government's help that they need, it would work better.

All agreed that it would need a change in the educators' mindset, which would be possible through proper training and awareness about this method of instruction. They further stated that the appropriate infrastructure, resources, etc. would be a big challenge and government support would be needed.

One of the big issues in Indian higher education institutes is large class sizes, which is even a bigger impediment to the flipped class teaching method, since educators have to move around and interact a lot with students. Although there is a policy to have 1:20 educator: student ratio, many classes have 60 or more students per class.

Lack of educator resources, especially those that are in this profession by choice and passion, was cited as another challenge and issue. One educator mentioned that though the term flipped learning is not used, he had experience with learning in this mode when doing his doctoral studies at a post-graduate institute, which he really enjoyed and felt that it was great for learning. However, for undergraduate programs, he doubted that it could be used effectively considering the large size of classes.

Another challenge for India is that students come from different social and economic backgrounds, with some being too poor to own personal laptops, which would be needed for proper viewing of digital content, video lectures, etc. However digitizing education is the trend and sooner or later the government has to deal with it and provide such resources for such students.

The suggestion that campuses would first need to be made Wi-Fi enabled was put forward as the first step, as most students own smartphones and also students could be provided with laptop subsidies, etc. One of them was very clear about the concept of flipped learning as he was already using it in his institute for many courses, though it was not called flipped learning. From his experience, he completely believes in this being the future of education, and mentioned that whether by force, policy, incentives, etc., this should be implemented in all universities over a period of time.

It was concluded that there is a lack of clarity among the key stakeholders, viz. educators, students, and administrators (institute management) about understanding the definition of flipped education. There is a need for identifying the key drivers and challenges for implementing flip education in higher education in India. Furthermore, the existing Indian education policy does not have a comprehensive policy framework for implementing flip education in institutes of higher learning in the country.

In a nutshell, all agreed that it should be implemented in colleges and universities, and unless the mindset of educators is changed, they are trained well, an adequate infrastructure is available, and government support and a clear policy frame is in place, it should not be "plunged" into right away. A step-wise introduction of flipped learning pedagogy use was suggested.

## 4.2 Key Drivers for the Adoption of Flipped Learning

The key drivers identified through the literature review, interviews, the visit to the college that has implemented flipped learning in India, and the focus group discussion helped to develop the questionnaire survey and to further collect data on these key drivers through questions formulated using either a Likert scale of 1-5 or multiple choice questions.

### 4.2.1 Findings and Descriptive Analysis

The questionnaire survey was the last step of the primary data collection for this research study, which was especially important for gathering primary data that at the time of this writing had not been conducted on educators' experience/perceptions of applying flipped learning pedagogy in higher education in India. From the interviews and focus group discussions it was obvious that many were not completely aware of flipped learning, few had experience with applying flipped learning, and some had only vague ideas about it. The multiple-choice and Likert scale questions made it convenient for participants to answer, and in addition limited the answer range in order to reduce outlier variables, and most importantly consumed less time to fill out and so helped to garner more responses.

The questionnaire survey (see Annex-1) was presented as a Google Form, which the respondents completed. The results are analyzed and interpreted in the next few sections. The survey was not anonymous (as Google Form collects the email IDs of respondents) to the researcher and in order to encourage the respondents to fill out the survey they were given the option of receiving the findings of this research. Notably, the respondents were informed in the survey itself what flipped learning was in order to avoid the confusion that surrounds the term and to ensure that every educator was operating under the same definition.

#### 4.2.1.1 Breakdown of Respondents

Of the 297 respondents of the survey, 54 percent were assistant professors, 25 percent were full professors, while 16 percent were associate professors. The remaining 15 percent were adjuncts, affiliates, and visiting educators and lecturers. More than two-thirds (68 percent) were male.

The age breakdown was diverse, with 8 percent of educators under the age of 29 and 7 percent of the professors over the age of 60. Most educators were in the middle of their careers, with 43 percent between the ages of 30 and 39, 26 percent between the ages of 40 and 49, and the remaining 16 percent between the ages of 50 and 59. The mean number of years of teaching experience was 13.5 years with a standard deviation of 9.5 years, suggesting a wide variety of teaching experience.

Lastly, the respondents were almost evenly split between those teaching at the bachelor (26 percent), master (39 percent), and doctoral levels (34 percent). Figure 4.5 depicts the breakdown of respondents' title, age, and teaching level.

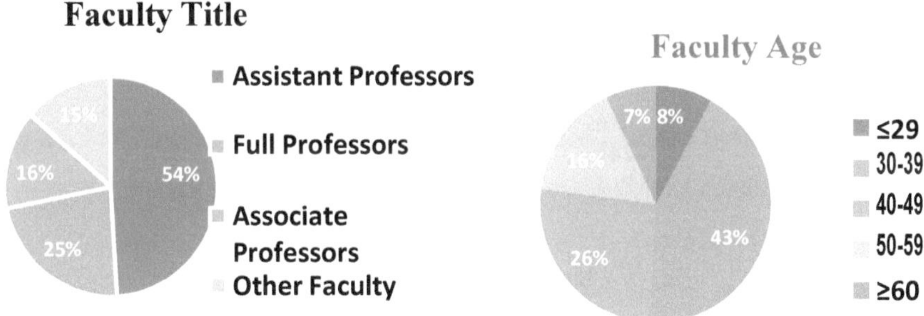


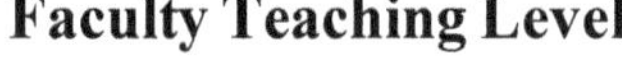


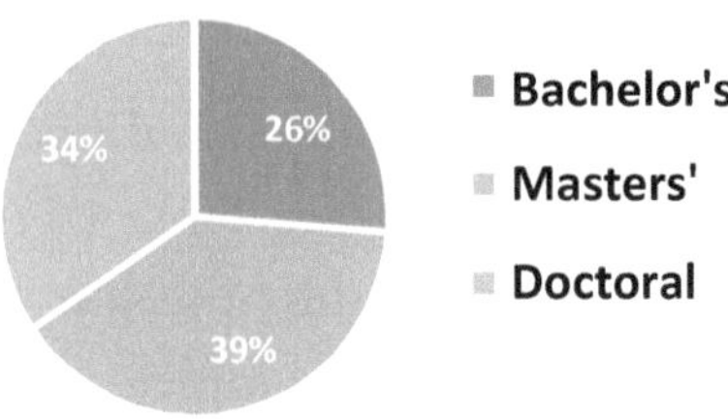


**Figure 4.5** Breakdown of Respondents

Overall, with more than 100 higher education institutions across India, and respondents across age, gender, and teaching experience and teaching level, this dataset is a unique insight into the views and future prospects of flipped learning in the context of Indian higher education. Appendix-E provides a list of the institutes/universities in India where the educators responded to the questionnaire survey.

#### 4.2.1.1 Awareness of Flipped Learning

Before analyzing flipped learning, it was crucial to understand how many college faculty members were aware of it and had actually "flipped a course." It was found that while 64 percent of the educators were aware of flipped learning/classrooms, only 21 percent had actually flipped a course (Figure 4.6). This suggests that even with widespread awareness, issues exist in implementing flipped learning in Indian higher education, due to which there is a lack of willingness on the part of both educators and institutes in adopting it.

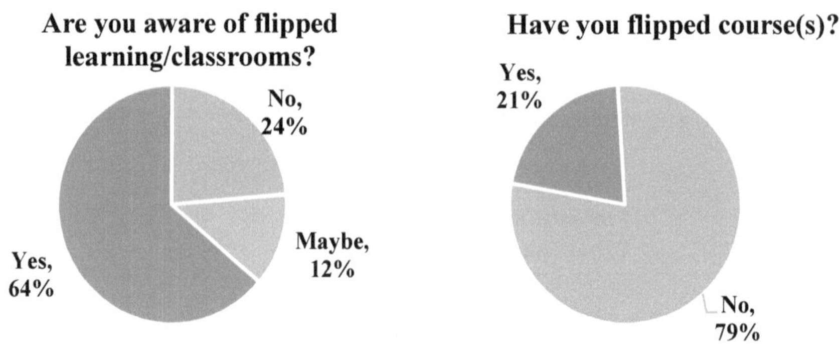


**Figure 4.6** Percentage of Educators Aware of and Experience with Flipped learning

Most educators did correctly identify that flipped learning encompasses a variety of different definitions (see Table 4.1). Of those respondents that did not correctly identify this, the most popular definition of flipped learning was that students "complete pre-class work individually before class and engage in teamwork and collaborative learning activities during class." However, only 6 percent of the respondents believed that the learning environment was designed to switch the focus away from the instructor and toward the students. This is not surprising in the context of Indian and more broadly Asian higher education systems, where the educators are often at the core of the learning experience.

**Table 4.1** Which Definition Aligns with Your Interpretation of Flipped Learning?

| Definition | No. of Respondents (in percentage) |
|---|---|
| The homework and lectures are reversed. Recorded lectures are viewed outside of class time, and homework is completed during class time | 7% |
| Students complete pre-class work individually before class and engage in teamwork and collaborative learning activities during class | 22% |
| Lectures are recorded as videos for students to view outside of class time freeing up time in class to engage in discussions and problem solving | 16% |
| The learning environment is designed to switch the focus away from the instructor and toward the students | 6% |
| Elements of all definitions above | 49% |

### 4.2.1.2 Experience with Flipping a Course

The educators in the survey that had flipped a course were asked to respond to five questions in order to better describe their experience with doing so. The questions were constructed to understand the educator's experience with teaching and preparing for a flipped course and how it impacted the effectiveness of their course. Most of these educators flipped courses at the bachelor (41 percent) and master (34 percent) level, while only 9 percent of educators flipped courses at the doctoral level. The results are summarized in Figure 4.7.

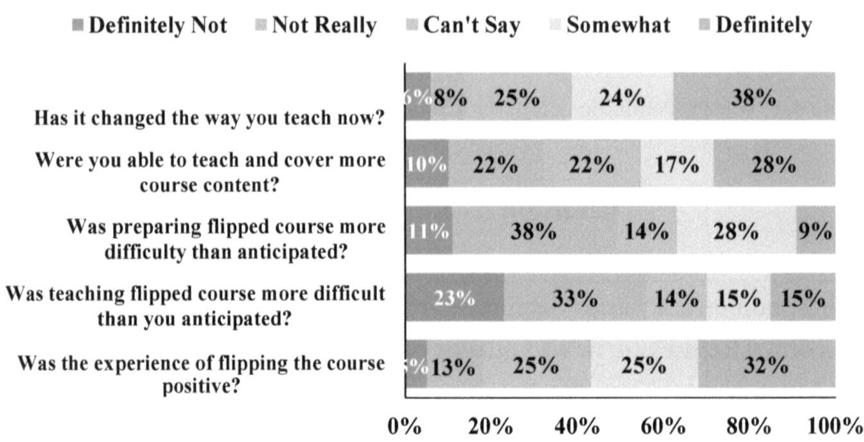


**Figure 4.7** Educator's Experience of Flipping Course

Based on the educators' responses, the experience of flipping courses has been overwhelmingly positive, with 57 percent of respondents finding that flipping courses was "definitely" or "somewhat" a positive experience and 62 percent of respondents finding it to change the way in which they teach now. In total, 37 percent of the respondents found that the preparation for using flipped learning was "somewhat" or "definitely" more difficult than anticipated. On the negative side, almost a third of the educators were unable to teach and cover more course contents (Figure 4.7).

Lastly, all of the educators were asked if they intended to flip a course in the future, and only 9 out of the sample of 297 (a negligible 3 percent) of the educators answered "no." This is a clear sign that flipped learning will grow further in India in the coming years (see Figure 4.8) and policy interventions at government and the institute administration level will be needed to help in this direction.

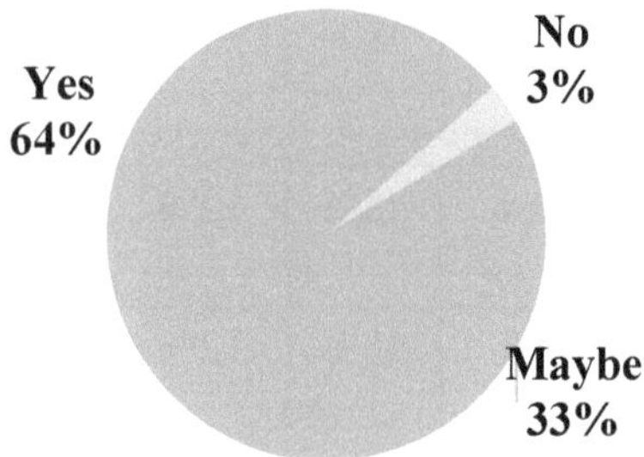


**Figure 4.8** Do You Intend to Flip a Course in the Future?

#### 4.2.1.3 Educator Perspective on Students in Flipped Learning

With flipped learning aimed at benefiting the students the most, the educators were asked to give their views on the students' perspectives of flipped learning. The questions could be responded to by indicating from strongly agree (a score of 5) or strongly disagree (a score of 1). The mean score between 1 and 5 was calculated for each question. Table 4.2 shows the results and sorted by the level of agreement with the statement.

It was found in Table 4.2 that the highest agreement was for students being comfortable using technology and asking more questions. The lowest level of agreement was that students preferred flipped learning and came to class prepared. These last two statements are linked. For flipped learning to work, students have to put in work at home and come to class prepared. If they do not want to do this, then they will prefer the traditional approach. On the positive side, 79 percent of the educators agreed or strongly agreed that the students were more engaged in class. This exhibits one of the key traits of flipped learning: engage students in their own learning.

**Table 4.2** Educators' Experience/Perception of Students' Perspectives of Flipped

| | Strongly Agree | Agree | Neither | Disagree | Strongly Disagree | Mean |
|---|---|---|---|---|---|---|
| (Response in percentage) | | | | | | |
| They are comfortable using technology | 28% | 48% | 12% | 6% | 5% | 3.85 |
| They ask more questions | 27% | 48% | 12% | 8% | 5% | 3.84 |
| They build relationships/ community feeling | 25% | 50% | 13% | 7% | 5% | 3.83 |
| They are more engaged in class | 21% | 58% | 6% | 8% | 7% | 3.78 |
| They are more collaborative | 18% | 54% | 15% | 8% | 5% | 3.72 |
| They see value of this type of experience | 20% | 49% | 18% | 8% | 5% | 3.71 |
| They adapt to the approach | 16% | 57% | 14% | 6% | 6% | 3.68 |
| Their grades are improved | 16% | 53% | 16% | 8% | 6% | 3.62 |
| They prefer it to the traditional approach | 18% | 45% | 14% | 16% | 6% | 3.50 |
| They come to class prepared | 16% | 43% | 17% | 15% | 7% | 3.40 |

### 4.2.1.4 Institutional Support

The "buy-in" of the institution is probably the first step in implementing flipped learning. Notably, only 28 percent of educators responded that their institution provided technical support, and 34 percent of the educators were provided with workshops and trainings on flipped learning. Only 33 percent of the educators were provided with a monetary or promotion incentive to teach a flipped learning course. Furthermore, only 35 percent of educators had their teaching load lowered to encourage the preparation of other flipped courses. Even though professors and students have positive views of flipped learning, without institutional support, it is difficult to implement it. In fact, it is clear that institutions need to be doing more to provide workshops and trainings on flipped learning and technical support if more professors are to implement it. While monetary or promotional incentives do not exist, this would be difficult to implement in the context of higher education, which tends to reward publishing/research more than teaching (Figure 4.9).

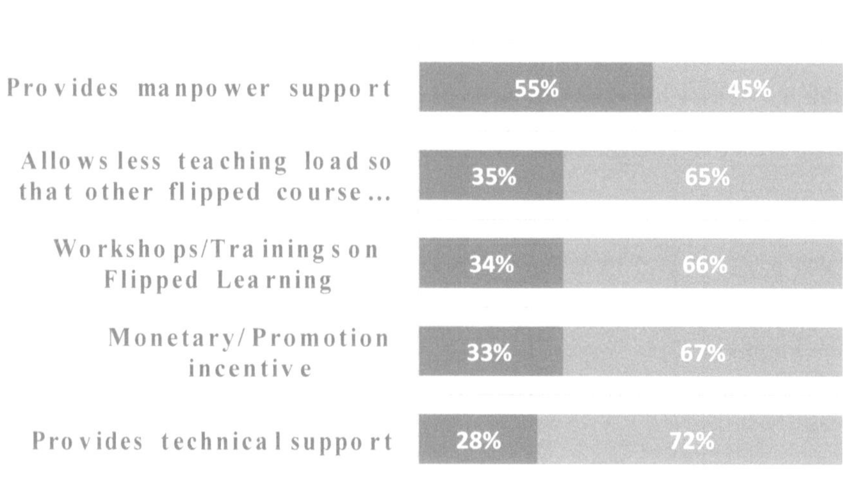


**Figure 4.9** Encouragement from Institute/Administration to Offer Flipped Learning

### 4.2.1.5 Challenges to Flip Courses

The educators were asked to indicate what challenges they would face if they had to flip courses. The educator could respond with the challenge being insignificant (1) or very significant (5). The mean of these values was then calculated in order to understand which challenges were most difficult (see Table 4.3).

Of all the challenges, *time* was the most often cited challenge faced by educators. In fact, 72 percent of the educators cited it as a moderate, significant, or very significant challenge. The highest percentage cited *time* as a challenge relative to the others. Experience with technology and the value perceived by colleagues and administration was cited as the least challenging hurdle to overcome by educators. Educators need to be creative and develop new ideas for flipped learning to be effective, and 47 percent responded that being creative and developing new ideas were a significant or very significant challenge. In the previous question, we learned that as little as 35 percent of educators had their teaching load lowered in order to encourage the preparation of other flipped courses. This insight, coupled with the fact that lack of time was cited as their biggest challenge, is an important note for higher education institutions and policymakers to keep in mind.

**Table 4.3** What Challenges Will Be Faced If You Have to Flip the Course?

| | Insignificant | Moderate | Can't Say | Significant | Very Significant | Mean Score |
|---|---|---|---|---|---|---|
| Time | 16% | 20% | 12% | 32% | 20% | 3.19 |
| Being creative/ developing new strategies and ideas | 18% | 20% | 15% | 29% | 18% | 3.09 |
| Lack of Support resources/ funding/Space | 16% | 21% | 22% | 22% | 20% | 3.09 |
| Other responsibilities required by my position | 20% | 14% | 21% | 28% | 18% | 3.08 |
| Competing department/ college/campus goals | 20% | 15% | 29% | 22% | 14% | 2.95 |
| Student resistance/lack of motivation | 16% | 21% | 28% | 25% | 11% | 2.94 |

| | | | | | | |
|---|---|---|---|---|---|---|
| Not understood by colleagues/ Administration | 20% | 14% | 33% | 21% | 12% | 2.90 |
| Not valued by colleagues/ Administration | 21% | 18% | 31% | 16% | 14% | 2.86 |
| My experience/ comfort with technology | 30% | 19% | 16% | 22% | 14% | 2.72 |

#### 4.2.1.6 The Indian Context

Since this dataset and survey are unique in that it is the first such a survey was developed for Indian educators' perspectives of adopting flipped learning as a pedagogy, it was important for educator to provide their views on flipped learning in the context of India. Figure 4.10 depicts a summary of the findings.

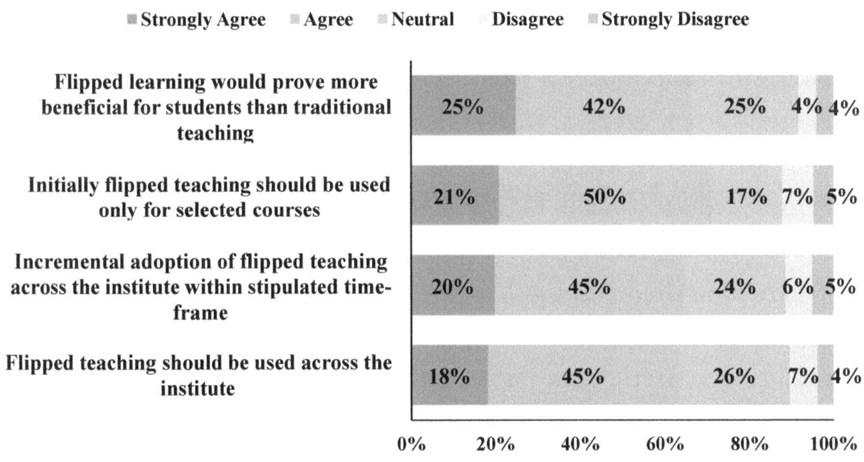


**Figure 4.10** Flipped Learning in the Context of India

In the Indian context, the educators' responses were overwhelmingly positive. Sixty-three percent of educators either "agreed" or "strongly agreed" that flipped learning should be used *across* their institutions, with 65 percent calling for it to be adopted across the institution within a stipulated time frame. Additionally, 67 percent believed that flipped learning is *more beneficial* than traditional learning. This level of optimism regarding flipped learning from educators was reassuring. That being said, a majority of educators (71 percent) did believe that flipped learning should only be implemented with select courses. Nevertheless, this suggests that flipped learning is highly implementable within the Indian higher education system.

### 4.2.2 Factor Analysis

Flipped learning has been popular for ten years as of the time of this writing, and it is beneficial in many ways for students that represent the future workforce in India. Still it has not been adopted as the pedagogy in Indian higher education institutes. In order to understand the reasons and causes behind this, factor analysis was performed on the rich data collected through the questionnaire survey in order to identify key drivers based on the educators' experience and perception of flipped learning in the context of India. A total of 297 educators' (from various backgrounds and in different age groups and professorial levels) responses from more than 100 universities/institutes (covering various categories such as deemed universities, institutes of national importance, public and private colleges) across India were gathered. These data were analyzed statistically by using SPSS 2.0 and by performing factor analysis, which resulted in five significant factors out of 25 key drivers that were identified and for which responses were gathered on a Likert scale. The five factors in the order of most leading factor to less leading were labeled as (i) students' improved learning outcome; (ii) institutional support through administrative support and incentives; (iii) convenience and flexibility in implementation; (iv) educators' satisfactory experience; and (v) flipped course preparation and delivery convenience.

A data adequacy check for the factor analysis was conducted using the Kaiser- Meyer-Olkin (KMO) test. Table 4.4 below presents the KMO and Barlett's test of the study. The data collected and the sampling mechanism were good, can be inferred if the KMO value for the model is greater than 0.6 (minimum requirement specified by Kinnear and Gray 1994), which in this case is 0.863, thus proceeded with factor analysis. Furthermore, the Barlett's test of sphericity was also significant (p=0.000). The principal component analysis and rotation method of varimax with Kaiser normalization resulted in rotation converging into five iterations or factors. All had factor loadings greater than standard threshold value of 0.6, as shown in Table 4.5, and so all were accepted resulting in five factors which were labeled and are described as follows.

**Table 4.4** KMO and Bartlett's Test

| | | |
|---|---|---|
| Kaiser-Meyer-Olkin Measure of Sampling Adequacy. | | .863 |
| Bartlett's Test of Sphericity | Approx. Chi-Square | 4419.306 |
| | Df | 300 |
| | Sig. | 0.000 |

**Table 4.5** Rotated Component Matrix[a]

| | Component | | | | |
|---|---|---|---|---|---|
| | 1 | 2 | 3 | 4 | 5 |
| Students are more collaborative in a flipped course | .848 | | | | |
| Students see value in the flipped learning experience | .831 | | | | |
| Students build relationships/community feeling in a flipped course | .829 | | | | |
| Students are comfortable using technology for a flipped course | .793 | | | | |
| Students come to class prepared for a flipped course | .791 | | | | |
| Students adapt to the flipped learning approach | .784 | | | | |
| Students ask more questions in a flipped course | .769 | | | | |

| | | | | | |
|---|---|---|---|---|---|
| Students Grades are improved in a flipped course | .738 | | | | |
| Students are more engaged in a flipped course | .700 | | | | |
| Students prefer a flipped course to a traditional approach | .675 | | | | |
| Students are not resistant to a flipped course | .624 | | | | |
| Manpower support is provided to encourage offering flipped learning | | .794 | | | |
| Technical support is provided to encourage offering flipped learning | | .779 | | | |
| Monetary incentive or promotion is provided to encourage offering flipped learning | | .767 | | | |
| Workshops/trainings are conducted to encourage offering flipped learning | | .744 | | | |
| Teaching loads are reduced to allow preparing for flipped learning | | .705 | | | |
| Flipped teaching can be implemented incrementally for all programs across the institute/university | | | .844 | | |
| Flipped teaching can be implemented across the programs in the institute/university | | | .755 | | |
| Flipped teaching can be implemented as it is more beneficial for students | | | .735 | | |
| Flipped teaching can only be applied to selected courses only | | | .730 | | |
| Flipped teaching is more interactive | | | | .820 | |
| Flipped courses cover more content | | | | .817 | |
| The experience of teaching a flipped course is positive | | | | .751 | |
| Preparing for a flipped course is convenient | | | | | .907 |
| Teaching a flipped course is convenient | | | | | .896 |

Extraction Method: Principal Component Analysis.

Rotation Method: Varimax with Kaiser Normalization.

a. Rotation converged in 5 iterations.

i. Students' Improved Learning Outcomes

The flipped learning pedagogy has proven to be beneficial for students with improved learning outcomes for those that undertake classes run in the flipped mode. The students are more collaborative as they have already developed prior understanding and knowledge with prior self-learning through presentations, videos, etc., and feel confident in discussing and presenting their views to their peers and the teacher during discussions. The students see value in the flipped learning experience as they find that doing self-study helps them to become life-long learners, which is a must in today's ever-fast changing developments (technical and innovative) taking place in all fields. With the active learning environment of the flipped classroom, the students are able to build relationships with their peers and develop community feeling. They help each other in the journey of learning together. The current generation is very techno savvy and very comfortable in using technology for flipped courses with ease, thus are able to adapt to the flipped learning approach effortlessly. They are eager to come prepared for class seeing the value of flipped learning, which requires prior knowledge to be able to participate in class activities enthusiastically. This preparation leads to students being more engaged in class, thus improving their grades and learning outcomes. With all of these benefits experienced by students they tend not to resist the flipped course and prefer it over traditional approaches as they feel more important in this student-centered approach of learning.

ii. Institutional Support through Administrative Support and Incentives

For the successful and effective implementation of flipped learning, it is very important that institutional support be extended to educators through administrative support and incentives. One of the ways is to provide manpower support in the form of teaching assistants that can assist with various in-class activities, and monitor and evaluate the students' progress to let them know the results right after the class, which can help the students improve by attending to the areas in which they are weak. The major concern faced by educators is preparing the course content in video format with intermittent quizzes, and uploading them in appropriate platforms, and if technical support is readily available, they are encouraged to offer flipped courses. The preparation and development of flipped courses require a considerable amount of time, which can be a demotivating factor unless some kind of monetary gain can be achieved or incentive in the form of giving more weightage for using flipped learning while evaluating for promotion to the next academic rank is considered. Furthermore, permitting the educators to participate in workshops/trainings on flipped learning will enable awareness amongst them, and also encourage them to try flipped courses. The workshops/trainings are useful, as educators do not have to spend time individually trying to figure out how to apply a flipped learning approach that is beneficial for students and the needs of the day in this digital world. However, since preparing for and developing flipped courses require an immense amount of time and effort, especially initially when doing it for the first time, it would be worthwhile if the teaching load were reduced for educators keen on applying flipped learning. The institutions thus need to strategize and provide support accordingly.

iii. Conveniences and Flexibility in Implementation

The flipped learning pedagogy concept is simple to understand, but in the absence of awareness of it, educators' impressions are that creating flipped courses is a huge task. However, the data collected indicate that almost all educators are ready to offer it in the future (with 64 percent saying "yes" and 33 percent saying "maybe" they will offer flipped courses in the future, and only 3% saying "no," which are those that are in the retirement age bracket). Thus, it can be inferred that if support is provided, they would be ready to offer a flipped course. The inherent flexibility and convenience in offering flipped learning make it implementable. Depending on the preparedness of the educators, the implementation can be done rapidly across all programs of the institute, or incrementally, or just for selected courses only as it can be applied to courses of varied subjects and areas. Flipped learning being beneficial for students and their learning outcomes makes it a motivating factor for implementing it. In the step-wise incremental introduction of flipped learning, the educators that are techno savvy and experienced in using active learning approaches, such as moderating group discussion, peer discussion, the case study method, gamification, etc. can first initiate offering flipped courses, and in the meantime the rest of the educators can be trained through workshops/trainings on flipped learning. Additionally, the experienced educators can take the lead in training their peers as well.

iv. Educators' Satisfactory Experience

The most important aspect of flipped learning is that it is an interactive and not a passive method of one-way teaching, where educators are not sure if the students are really absorbing the knowledge being communicated or are mere listeners. The upbeat experience of shared and collaborative teaching and learning is a major motivator for an educator to apply flipped learning. Furthermore, flipped learning by design requires educators to plan and organize the course well in advance. This is owing to the fact that video lectures need to be recorded prior to class. The controlled environment of the recording studio, without any distraction, helps in covering more content in the allocated time and in an organized manner, with an additional benefit for students to review the content even later again for better understanding, and that too at their convenience. This is not possible in traditional teaching where educators are often found rushing to cover the course content. The educators' positive experience with teaching flipped courses becomes a motivating factor for them to use and apply this pedagogy for their courses.

v. Flipped Course Preparation and Delivery Convenience

Preparing and delivering flipped courses are convenient, though in the beginning educators may find it time consuming. However in the long run this becomes convenient, with educators needing to only improvise the course content with very little effort. The educator does not need to repeat the lectures day after day, which can become very boring for them. Further, depending on the students' understanding and response during the class, the educator can adjust the learning strategies to make the teaching/learning more effective.

## 4.3 Challenges Faced in Adoption of Flipped Learning in Higher Education in India

The main objective of this study was to identify the challenges in adopting flipped learning pedagogy by educators in higher education institutes in India. With the understanding developed through the literature review, interviews, and case study, a focus group discussion was held where educators and the researcher concluded in consensus the following eleven factors identified as challenges faced by the educators in applying flipped learning as a pedagogy for higher education.

i. Lack of time

ii. Competing department goals

iii. Lack of institutional support

iv. Lack of incentives

v. Lack of educator's skills

vi. Inadequate workshops/trainings

vii. Lack of recognition

viii. Student's resistance

ix. Large class size

x. Educator's resistance

xi. Lack of management awareness

### 4.3.1 Total Interpretative Structural Modeling

In order to model the challenges identified in adopting the flipped learning pedagogy by educators in higher education institutes in India, the Total Interpretive Structural Modeling technique was used, which is very useful for qualitative study when trying to establish relationships, build up relationships, and discover the causality. With the understanding developed through the literature review, interviews, and case study, followed by focus group discussion, the challenges faced by the educators in applying flipped learning as a pedagogy for higher education were identified. The modeling of the challenges carried out provides the structure showing the relationships among the challenges identified, and accordingly a suggestive framework was recommended. For this the first step was to explain the challenges identified, as given below.

i. Lack of Time

'Lack of time' has been listed as one of the biggest barriers faced by educators in applying flipped learning (Shnai, 2017). Various researchers have conducted interviews for their studies on flipped learning and the educators have always opined the lack of time as one of the barriers in adopting the flipped learning approach for teaching. The educators in India hardly have any spare time, and the thought of designing and creating new content could be enough to turn even the most enthusiastic of educators off (Ram & Sinha, 2017). Flipped learning requires time and effort to prepare and organize lecture content that is suitable for active learning based activities and that motivates students to prepare for engaging in classroom activities (Bergmann and Sams 2012; Hamdan et al. 2013; Milman 2013; as cited in Lee, Lim, and Kim 2017). Additionally, inside class active learning based activities requires both time and effort to develop them in a way that it motivates students to prepare for classroom activities and provides them with interactive learning experience, which is important factor for successful flipped learning outcome. (Arum et al. 2012; McLaughlin et al. 2014 as cited in Lee, Lim, and Kim 2017). Educators also need to "create an alternative assessment for learners to elicit and demonstrate their knowledge according to the prescribed learning outcomes" (Bergmann & Sams, 2014). As a result, introducing a flip means that educator needs to acquire relevant IT as well as creative skills and pursue strategies which is an additional work that requires a considerable amount of time, which is lacking amongst educators with additional responsibilities that they need to perform, such as conducting sponsored and research projects, publishing, consultancy, outreach activities, etc.

ii. Competing Department Goals

Competing departmental goals has not been specifically quoted as a challenge in any of the literature reviews done for this study, and this indicates that educators have more flexibility, freedom, and resources to apply any pedagogical approach that they believe in. However, this came up during the focus group discussion with the seven educators from different higher education institutes across India. It was pointed out that educators have an obligation to carry out research work, outreach activities, administrative jobs assigned from time-to-time, conduct conferences, etc. These are in addition to teaching and the objectives and goals set up by the educators' department, towards which they have to work as part of their responsibility. The primary data collected through the questionnaire survey for this study also indicated that 80% of the educators found it a challenge (ranging from moderate to a very significant challenge).

iii. Lack of Institutional Support

Educators face scarcity of resources while preparing, developing and implementing flipped classrooms (Shnai, 2017). Lack of institutional support was identified as one of the challenges for implementing flipped learning pedagogy during the focus group discussion conducted by the researcher for this study. Additionally, the primary data collected indicated that 84% of the educators in India found it a challenge (ranging from a moderate to a very significant challenge) in adopting flipped learning with only 16% finding it an insignificant challenge. Resources are needed in the form of technical support, such as an appropriate learning management system (LMS) and also manpower support to provide the needed assistance in using these and in preparing and uploading video lectures that have a quiz as a component, and other contents online for the use of the students. Manpower support would also be needed in monitoring and evaluating online quizzes, etc. Unless proper technical and manpower systems are in place, the implementation of flipped learning can be hampered. All of this requires fund allocation in order to create appropriate infrastructure facilities for this purpose.

iv. Lack of Incentives (Monetary/Promotional)

The primary data collected through the questionnaire survey for this study indicated that only 33% (against 67%) opined that they received monetary/promotional incentives to adopt flipped learning pedagogy. This is not at all encouraging for educators, especially when they have to put in additional time and effort, without much institutional support, to apply flipped learning pedagogy, making students the recipients of the benefits of learning outcomes that stem from flipped learning. None of the research papers reviewed highlighted that educators had received monetary or promotional incentives, and it seems that educators adopt it for their professional satisfaction, knowing that it will be beneficial for their students' learning. The incentives however, if provided, can have a greater impact on flipped learning being adopted by educators even if it means using additional time and effort on their own.

Lack of Individual Skills (being creative, developing new ideas and strategies)

The lack of skills required for developing flipped courses can lead to disinterest amongst educators in adopting the flipped learning pedagogical approach, even if they believe that it would be beneficial for students learning outcomes and would be fruitful. The educators are used to traditional learning that they have themselves experienced as learners, and flipped learning is completely new for them. In a traditional setting, an educator needs to deliver a lecture in class with hardly any interactive session with students, and then he or she just evaluates students based on their assignments, project work, quizzes, and mid-term and final examinations. Developing flipped courses requires skills that vary from technical ICT skills to soft skills, being creative to having new ideas and strategies to design flipped courses in order to provide interactive learning experiences (McLaughlin et al., 2014): "Most importantly, the design needs to create a tight link between what students do in class and what they do at home" (Stannard 2012). The primary data collected for this study through the questionnaire survey indicated that a large 82% of the educators found a lack of their skills as a challenge (ranging from a moderate to a very significant challenge) with only 18% of the educators stating that it was an insignificant challenge.

v. Inadequate Workshop/Trainings

The main criticism of the flipped classroom approach was the lack of trained educators for this approach, which definitely requires revision in the curricula of the education faculties, which includes information about the flipped classroom approach and training courses on it (Serin & Khabibullin, 2019). Many educators while possibly having the skills to develop student-centered learning content suitable for flipped learning may not have the training or experience to put this into effect in the classroom (Lakshmi et al., 2017). During the interviews and exploring this topic in Indian context, it was found that though some educators have had experience with flipping a class give presentations in their home institutes in order to share their experience of flipping the course with their colleagues, there are hardly any workshops/trainings with concerted a focus on flipped learning available for the educators to attend. The findings of the primary data collected through questionnaire survey also were in line with this, as a massive 66% of the educators negatively responded to the relevant workshops/trainings available for flipped learning or those that were being conducted and which they were encouraged to attend. While the idea of flipped classrooms is straightforward and easy to initiate, careful and elaborate preparation is desirable for effective results: "Haphazard implementation may result in compromised learning environments with troubled faculty and unsatisfied students" (Ram & Sinha, 2017). Thus, it is imperative to organize well-planned workshops/trainings for the educators that are interested in using the flipped learning approach.

vi. Lack of Recognition

The findings of the primary data collected through the questionnaire survey indicated that 80% of the educators found that flipped learning was not understood by their colleagues and the administration, and 79% of the educators indicated that it was not valued by the colleagues/administration, with only 20% and 21% respectively stating that this was an insignificant challenge. If it is neither understood nor valued by colleagues/administration, then it is obvious that even educators that are keen on trying and applying flipped learning for their courses may feel discouraged to do so in the absence of any recognition. The prevalent misunderstanding is that in the flipped learning model the role of the educator is substituted or minimized by the videos. Salman Khan, who runs the Khan Academy, stated that on the contrary, the educator has a superior role requiring the conducting of higher learning activities by managing interactive simulations and labs with students, carrying out individual intervention, and simplifying peer-to-peer learning (Khan, 2011), which should demand recognition because of the amount of time and effort educators put into it.

vii. Students' Resistance

For flipped learning to work, students have to work on their own prior to class in order to gain knowledge. Of course the content to be used for this is provided by the educator, but students have to understand this prerequisite of the flipped classroom, which prepares them to actively participate in all of the activities planned by the educator for the inside class sessions. However, in various studies conducted, the educators have pointed out that students do not come to class prepared, which hampers the effectiveness of flipped learning. It was found that one reason for this is the unfamiliarity of the flipped learning concept amongst learners (students) and what is expected of them (Shnai, 2017). Another study made observations about the students' inability to learn independently, especially undergraduate students that were less motivated and committed than postgraduate students in terms of putting an effort into learning on their own (Lakshmi et al., 2017). As similar observation was noted: "Students may require a gradual introduction to flipped learning over time, as well as explicit support to develop particular attributes (such as self-directed learning skills) to enhance their readiness for the student-centered nature of flipped classrooms" (Hao, 2016). While it is assumed that lectures may be boring and that students are not keen to watch them, it was found that even if the lectures are of good quality, students may not view or comprehend them, perhaps due to distractions online, a lack of self- regulation, or inadequate live support by the instructor (Bergmann and Sams 2012; Hamdan et al. 2013; Milman 2013; as cited in Lee, Lim, and Kim 2017).

viii. Large Class Size

Large class sizes are a typical problem in institutes of higher education in India, especially in undergraduate courses, where on an average at least 60 students sit in class at any given time, and it may go up to 100-150 students. This again was not reported in any of the findings of the research papers that were reviewed for this study, which is understandable since the studies conducted were either in western countries or countries with a comparatively smaller cohort of young adults comprising the share of the population. This is increased by the ever mushrooming of the higher education institutes while the number of qualified educators remains inadequate in India. Flipped learning requires close interaction and vigilance in class by the educator, who has to interact with different groups working in class on various discussions or activities. However, flipped learning is also cited as convenient to use for large class sizes, and it has been suggested that students can use class time effectively for discussion or class activities with smaller groups formed amongst peers (Aronson & Arfstrom, 2013).

ix. Individual Resistance

Flipped learning is a new phenomenon, which was not experienced by educators when they were learners themselves. Thus, most educators still are ignorant of this pedagogical approach and the rest feel that it is not worth spending their scarce time and effort on experimenting with flipped classrooms. They have a very rigid view that traditional learning is appropriate and lectures should be delivered face to face in class with the students being able to clarify their doubts if needed. During the focus group discussion it was observed that the senior educators were especially resistant. The primary data collected through cohort questionnaire survey indicated that 79% had not ever flipped a course, and only 21% had tried it. However, 64% of the educators noted that they intend to flip courses in future, with 36% stating that they may or may not do so.

x. Lack of Management Awareness

During the interviews conducted with several directors/senior administrators of the higher education institutes in India, it was clear that they either are not aware of flipped learning, or support blended learning, thinking that it is a step towards flipped learning. The focus is more on producing graduates with the technical and specialized skills required for industries rather than graduates with personalities that can fit a varied job markets, possessing life-long learning attitudes and capabilities. Unless, the management is aware of the benefits that flipped learning pedagogy has on students' learning experience and outcomes, the move in the direction of adopting flipped learning pedagogy by top-level administration will not materialize. It is obvious from one of the private colleges in India that was visited for the case study purposes that unless the top administration is supportive and willing to plunge into the new initiative, it is next to impossible to implement. None of the research papers reviewed for this study highlighted this aspect, but it is obvious from the two examples, one in India and one in Turkey, where the flipped learning approach was adopted across the institute for all of its programs offerings, that it was the will and support of the top management that made it possible to implement it successfully.

#### 4.3.1.1 Methodology for Challenges Identification and Validation

I. Identification of Challenges

A set of seven significant variables or challenges was identified through the literature review and was discussed in the previous section. Table 4.6 summarizes the supporting literature on the identified variables.

**Table 4.6** Literature for the Identified Variables

| S. No | Variables/Challenges | Literature Support |
|---|---|---|
| 1. | Lack of Time | Arum et al. 2012; Bergmann and Sams 2012; Hamdan et al. 2013; Milman 2013; McLaughlin et al. 2014; Bergmann & Sams, 2014; Lee et al., 2017; Ram and Sinha 2017; Shnai 2017 |
| 2. | Competing Department Goals | Author's primary data - focus group discussion |
| 3. | Lack of Institutional Support | Shnai 2017 |
| 4. | Lack of Incentives | Author's primary data - focus group discussion |
| 5. | Lack of Individual Skills | Stannard 2012; McLaughlin et al. 2014 |
| 6. | Inadequate Workshops/Trainings | Lakshmi et al. 2017; Ram and Sinha 2017; Serin and Khabibullin 2019 |
| 7. | Lack of Recognition | Khan, 2011 |
| 8. | Student's Resistance | Bergmann and Sams 2012; Hamdan et al. 2013; Milman 2013; Hao 2016; Lakshmi et al. 2017; Lee, Lim, and Kim 2017; Shnai, 2017 |
| 9. | Large Class Size | Aronson & Arfstrom, 2013 |
| 10. | Individual Resistance | Author's primary data - focus group discussion |
| 11. | Lack of Management Awareness | Author's primary data - focus group discussion |

II Validation of Variables

The set of seven variables identified through the literature review was validated with the help of the primary data collection and expert opinions. In addition, four more variables, namely competing department goals, lack of incentives, educator's resistance, and lack of management awareness, emerged during the personal interviews with several top administrators of academic institutes, faculty members of higher education, and a focus group discussion with seven faculty members from different categories of higher education institutes in India. Primary data were collected through administering a structured online questionnaire survey to the faculty members of higher education institutes across India.

All eleven identified challenges were then again validated from the five experts (educators) from five different institutes of higher education in India. The contextual relationships among the identified challenges were established through a focus group discussion conducted with these five educators anonymously. Based on their opinions, the eleven variables were finalized, which were then modeled through Total Interpretive Structural Modeling, which is a qualitative data analysis technique (Dubey et al., 2016; Sanjay Prasad et al. 2018).

## 4.3.2 TISM Methodology and Model Development

TISM is an extension of Interpretive Structural Modeling (ISM), which is a qualitative technique of structuring a set of different and related variables into a comprehensive contextual model (Dubey et al., 2016; Sanjay Prasad et al. 2018). It generally has the following steps (Dubey et al., 2016; Mahajan R.et al. 2016; J. Jena et al. 2016; Sanjay Prasad et al. 2018), shown pictorially in Figure 4.11 on the following page.

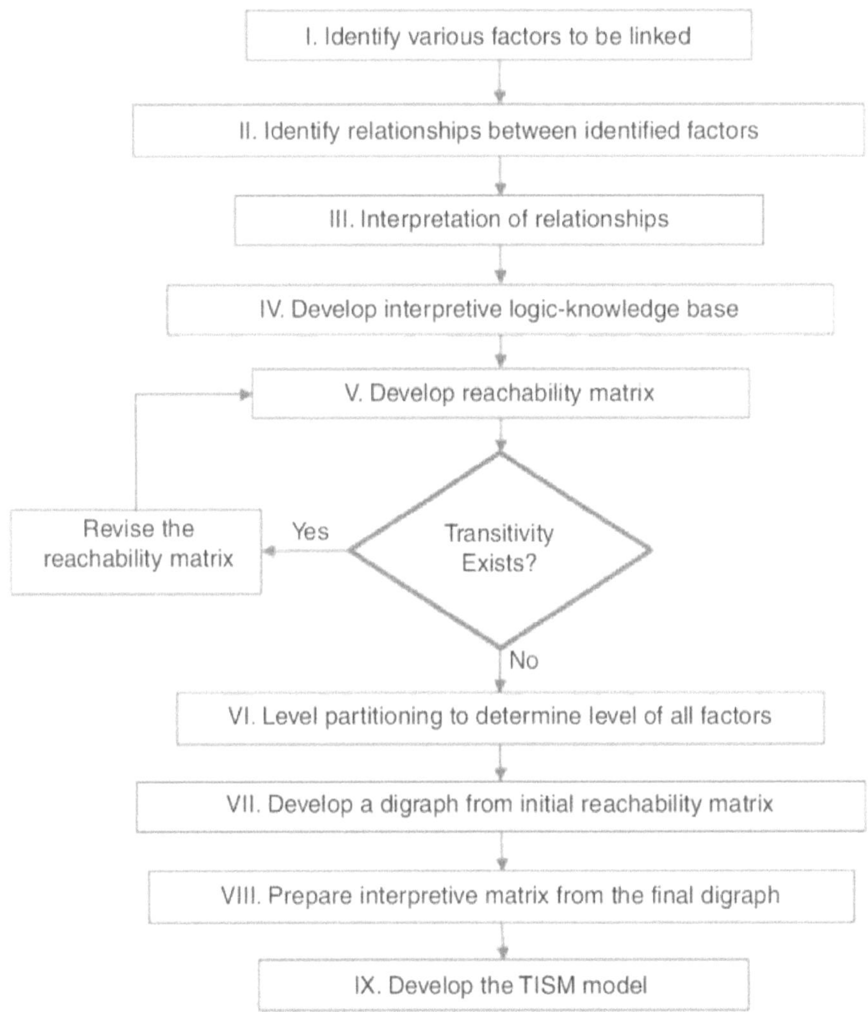


**Figure 4.11** Basic Steps Involved in TISM

*Source: Modified from Sushil (2005), Downloaded by Dr. Sanjay Prasad, 21 September 2018 (PT)*

## Step 1: Identification and listing of the relevant variables

The relevant challenges are identified and validated as mentioned in the previous section.

### Step 2: Defining contextual relationships

The relationships among the identified challenges were established by understanding whether a particular challenge influenced other challenges in the form of a "lead to" type of relation.

### Step 3: Interpretive logic-knowledge base

In this stage, the aim is to identify contextual relationships with relevant logic among the listed variables in the form of pairwise comparison. During the focus group discussion, experts' opinions were sought in order to compare one identified challenge against another identified challenge. For each comparison of one challenge with another one (in terms of the "lead to" type relationship), each expert needed to give a reply in the form of "Yes" or "No.". The responses of each expert were noted, along with the logical reason for their reply. The response given by the majority of the experts was considered for inclusion in the table. Following this methodology, the interpretive logic-knowledge base was obtained showing the complete set of comparisons (110 comparisons for 11 variables) as listed in Table 4.7.

### Step 4: Development of a reachability matrix from the Contextual Relationships and then scrutinize the matrix for transitivity

A reachability matrix was developed by using the interpretive logic-knowledge base formed in step 3 above, by following the below mentioned rule:

Wherever *i-j* entry is 'Yes', 1 is entered in the i-j cell of the matrix
Wherever *i-j* entry is 'No', 0 is entered in the i-j cell of the matrix

Thereafter, the reachability matrix (Table 4.8) was checked for transitivity. The rule followed for checking transitivity is that if Variable A leads to Variable B and Variable B leads to Variable C, then Variable A should lead to Variable C also (Singh MD et al. 2003; J. Jena et al. 2016; Sanjay Prasad et al. 2018). Upon identification, the transitivity was included at required places in the reachability matrix and a final reachability matrix (Table 4.9) was obtained. Accordingly, the interpretive logic-knowledge base was updated for each new transitive link by changing the relevant "No" entry to "Yes*" and writing the word "Transitive" in front of them in the interpretation column (Sushil 2005; Singh MD et al. 2003; Mahajan R. et.al. 2016).

### Step 5: Carrying out level partitioning of the reachability matrix

Level partitioning of the variables was done in a step-by-step manner. The reachability and antecedent sets were identified for each variable, where the reachability set consisted of the variable itself and the other variables that led it, while the antecedent set consisted of the variable itself and the other variables it led to. For the purpose of allotting levels to each variable, an intersection set was derived and whenever the reachability set and intersection set was the same, a level was allotted to that variable and the variable was removed from the list for further level partitioning. In the current study, it took 6 iterations to achieve levels for all of the variables. Accordingly, each level partition table was placed in Table 4.10 to Table 4.16 and finally the complete level-wise partition was placed in Table 4.17.

**Table 4.7** Interpretive Logic – Knowledge Base

| | Variable No. | Paired Comparison of Challenges | Yes/ No | Justification (In what way will one challenge lead to another challenge?) |
|---|---|---|---|---|
| **C1-Lack of Time** | | | | |
| 1. | C1-C11 | Lack of time leads to a lack of management awareness. | No | |
| 2. | C11-C1 | Lack of management awareness leads to a lack of time. | Yes* | Transitive |
| **3.** | **C1-C10** | **Lack of time leads to the educator's resistance.** | **Yes** | **An innovative approach needs time.** |

| | | | | |
|---|---|---|---|---|
| 4. | C10-C1 | Educator's resistance leads to a lack of time. | No | |
| 5. | C1-C9 | Lack of time leads to a large class size. | No | |
| 6. | C9-C1 | Large class size leads to a lack of time. | No | |
| 7. | C1-C8 | Lack of time leads to students' resistance | Yes* | Transitive |
| 8. | C8-C1 | Students' resistance leads to a lack of time. | No | |
| 9. | C1-C7 | Lack of time leads to a lack of recognition. | Yes * | Transitive |
| 10. | C7-C1 | Lack of recognition leads to a lack of time. | Yes* | Transitive |
| 11. | C1-C6 | Lack of time leads to inadequate workshops/trainings. | No | |
| **12.** | **C6-C1** | **Inadequate workshops/trainings leads to a lack of time.** | **Yes** | **Required training helps in time management.** |
| **13.** | **C1-C5** | **Lack of time leads to a lack of the educator's skills.** | **Yes** | **Skill enhancement needs time.** |
| **14.** | **C5-C1** | **Lack of the educator's skills leads to a lack of time.** | **Yes** | **Required skills need more time.** |
| 15. | C1-C4 | Lack of time leads to a lack of incentives. | No | |
| 16. | C4-C1 | Lack of incentives leads to a lack of time. | Yes* | Transitive |
| 17. | C1-C3 | Lack of time leads to a lack of institutional support. | No | |

| | | | | |
|---|---|---|---|---|
| **18.** | **C3-C1** | **Lack of institutional support leads to a lack of time.** | **Yes** | **Need to spend more time** |
| 19. | C1-C2 | Lack of time leads to competing department goals. | No | |
| **20.** | **C2-C1** | **Competing department goals leads to a lack of time.** | **Yes** | **The educator remains busy in other department activities.** |
| **C2 Competing Department Goals** | | | | |
| 21. | C2-C11 | Competing department goals leads to a lack of management awareness. | No | |
| **22.** | **C11-C2** | **Lack of management awareness leads to competing department goals.** | **Yes** | **No interest in reforming traditional teaching approach** |
| **23.** | **C2-C10** | **Competing department goals lead to the educator's resistance.** | **Yes** | **Educators feel disoriented.** |
| 24. | C10-C2 | The educator's resistance leads to competing department goals. | No | |
| **25.** | **C2-C9** | **Competing department goals leads to a large class size.** | **Yes** | **The department gets more revenue from a greater number of students.** |
| 26. | C9-C2 | Large class size leads to competing department goals. | No | |

| | | | | |
|---|---|---|---|---|
| 27. | C2-C8 | Competing department goals leads to student's resistance. | Yes* | Transitive |
| 28. | C8-C2 | The student's resistance leads to competing department goals. | No | |
| **29.** | **C2-C7** | **Competing department goals lead to a lack of recognition.** | **Yes** | **The completion of assigned tasks only gets appreciation.** |
| 30. | C7-C2 | Lack of recognition leads to competing department goals. | No | |
| **31.** | **C2-C6** | **Competing department goals lead to inadequate workshops/trainings.** | **Yes** | **Different priorities** |
| 32. | C6-C2 | Inadequate workshops/trainings lead to competing dept. goals. | No | |
| **33.** | **C2-C5** | **Competing department goals lead to a lack of the educator's skills.** | **Yes** | **Different inclinations** |
| 34. | C5-C2 | The educator's skills lead to competing department goals. | No | |
| **35.** | **C2-C4** | **Competing department goals leads to a lack of incentives.** | **Yes** | **The accomplishment of department- defined goals gets associated rewards.** |

| | | | | |
|---|---|---|---|---|
| 36. | C4-C2 | Lack of incentives leads to competing department goals. | No | |
| **37.** | **C2-C3** | **Competing department goals lead to a lack of institutional support.** | **Yes** | **Institute resources are allocated for department priorities.** |
| 38. | C3-C2 | Lack of institutional support leads to competing department goals. | No | |
| **C3 Lack of Institutional Support** | | | | |
| 39. | C3-C11 | Lack of institutional support leads to a lack of management awareness. | No | |
| **40.** | **C11-C3** | **Lack of management awareness leads to a lack of institutional support.** | **Yes** | **Different priorities** |
| **41.** | **C3-C10** | **Lack of institutional support leads to the educator's resistance.** | **Yes** | **Educators do not gain motivation** |
| 42. | C10-C3 | The educator's resistance leads to a lack of institutional support. | No | |
| 43. | C3-C9 | Lack of institutional support leads to large class size. | No | |
| 44. | C9-C3 | Large class size leads to a lack of institutional support. | No | |

| | | | | |
|---|---|---|---|---|
| 45. | C3-C8 | Lack of institutional support leads to the student's resistance. | Yes* | Transitive |
| 46. | C8-C3 | The student's resistance leads to a lack of institutional support. | No | |
| **47.** | **C3-C7** | **Lack of institutional support leads to a lack of recognition.** | **Yes** | **No appreciation for innovative efforts** |
| 48. | C7-C3 | Lack of recognition leads to a lack of institutional support. | No | |
| **49.** | **C3-C6** | **Lack of institutional support leads to inadequate workshops/trainings.** | **Yes** | **Needs not realized** |
| 50. | C6-C3 | Inadequate workshops/trainings lead to lack of institutional support. | No | |
| **51.** | **C3-C5** | **Lack of institutional support leads to a lack of the educator's skills.** | **Yes** | **Need not recognized** |
| 52. | C5-C3 | Lack of the educator's skills leads to a lack of institutional support. | No | |
| **53.** | **C3-C4** | **Lack of institutional support leads to a lack of incentives.** | **Yes** | **Necessity not felt** |
| 54. | C4-C3 | Lack of incentives leads to lack of institutional support. | No | |

| C4 Lack of Incentives | | | | |
|---|---|---|---|---|
| 55. | C4-C11 | Lack of incentives leads to a lack of management awareness. | No | |
| **56.** | **C11-C4** | **Lack of management awareness leads to a lack of incentives.** | **Yes** | **The expectations of management are different.** |
| **57.** | **C4-C10** | **Lack of incentives leads to the educator's resistance.** | **Yes** | **No tangible or intangible benefits for educators** |
| 58. | C10-C4 | The educator's resistance leads to a lack of incentives. | No | |
| 59. | C4-C9 | Lack of incentives leads to a large class size. | No | |
| 60. | C9-C4 | Large class size leads to a lack of incentives. | No | |
| 61. | C4-C8 | Lack of incentives leads to the student's resistance. | Yes* | Transitive |
| 62. | C8-C4 | The student's resistance leads to a lack of incentives. | No | |
| 63. | C4-C7 | Lack of incentives leads to a lack of recognition. | Yes* | Transitive |
| **64.** | **C7-C4** | **Lack of recognition leads to a lack of incentives.** | **Yes** | **Interdependent** |
| 65. | C4-C6 | Lack of incentives leads to inadequate workshops/trainings. | No | |

| | | | | |
|---|---|---|---|---|
| 66. | C6-C4 | Inadequate workshops/trainings leads to a lack of incentives. | No | |
| **67.** | **C4-C5** | **Lack of incentive leads to a lack of the educator's skills.** | **Yes** | **No motivation for skills updating** |
| 68. | C5-C4 | Lack of the educator's skills leads to a lack of incentives. | Yes* | Transitive |
| **C5 Lack of Educator's Skills** | | | | |
| 69. | C5-C11 | Lack of the educator's skills leads to a lack of management awareness. | No | |
| **70.** | **C11-C5** | **Lack of management awareness leads to a lack of the educator's skills.** | **Yes** | **Importance of skill enhancement not recognized** |
| **71.** | **C5-C10** | **Lack of the educator's skills leads to the educator's resistance.** | **Yes** | **Fear of failure** |
| 72. | C10-C5 | The educator's resistance leads to a lack of the educator's skills. | No | |
| 73. | C5-C9 | Lack of the educator's skills leads to a large class size. | No | |
| 74. | C9-C5 | Large class size leads to a lack of the educator's skills. | No | |

| 75. | C5-C8 | Lack of the educator's skills leads to the student's resistance. | No | |
|---|---|---|---|---|
| 76. | C8-C5 | The student's resistance leads to a lack of the educator's skills. | No | |
| **77.** | **C5-C7** | **Lack of the educator's skills leads to a lack of recognition.** | **Yes** | **Worthy and relevant skills are appreciated.** |
| **78.** | **C7-C5** | **Lack of recognition leads to a lack of the educator's skills.** | **Yes** | **No motivation for skills improvement** |
| 79. | C5-C6 | Lack of the educator's skills leads to inadequate workshops/trainings. | No | |
| **80.** | **C6-C5** | **Inadequate workshops/trainings lead to a lack of the educator's skills.** | **Yes** | **Unavailability of platform to hone skills** |
| **C6 Inadequate Workshops/Trainings** | | | | |
| 81. | C6-C11 | Inadequate workshops/trainings lead to a lack of management awareness. | No | |
| **82.** | **C11-C6** | **Lack of management awareness leads to inadequate workshops/trainings.** | **Yes** | **Different priorities** |

| **83.** | **C6-C10** | **Inadequate workshops/trainings lead to the educator's resistance.** | **Yes** | **Educators remains hesitant to adopt new methods** |
|---|---|---|---|---|
| 84. | C10-C6 | The educator's resistance leads to inadequate workshops/trainings. | No | |
| 85. | C6-C9 | Inadequate workshops/ trainings leads to a large class size. | No | |
| 86. | C9-C6 | Large class size leads to inadequate workshops/trainings. | No | |
| 87. | C6-C8 | Inadequate workshops/trainings lead to the student's resistance. | Yes* | Transitive |
| 88. | C8-C6 | The student's resistance leads to inadequate workshops/trainings. | No | |
| 89. | C6-C7 | Inadequate workshops/trainings lead to a lack of recognition. | Yes* | Transitive |
| 90. | C7-C6 | Lack of recognition leads to inadequate workshops/trainings. | No | |
| **C7 Lack of Recognition** | | | | |
| 91. | C7-C11 | Lack of recognition leads to a lack of management awareness. | No | |

| | | | | |
|---|---|---|---|---|
| **92.** | **C11-C7** | **Lack of management awareness leads to a lack of recognition.** | **Yes** | **Indifferent attitude of management** |
| **93.** | **C7-C10** | **Lack of recognition leads to the educator's resistance.** | **Yes** | **Dearth of motivation** |
| 94. | C10-C7 | The educator's resistance leads to a lack of recognition. | No | |
| 95. | C7-C9 | Lack of recognition leads to a large class size. | No | |
| 96. | C9-C7 | Large class size leads to a lack of recognition. | No | |
| 97. | C7-C8 | Lack of recognition leads to the student's resistance. | Yes* | Transitive |
| 98. | C8-C7 | The student's resistance leads to a lack of recognition. | No | |
| **C8 Student's Resistance** | | | | |
| 99. | C8-C11 | The student's resistance leads to a lack of management awareness. | No | |
| 100. | C11-C8 | Lack of management awareness leads to the student's resistance. | Yes* | Transitive |
| **101.** | **C8-C10** | **The student's resistance leads to the educator's resistance.** | **Yes** | **Hostile class environment** |

| | | | | |
|---|---|---|---|---|
| 102. | C10-C8 | The educator's resistance leads to the student's resistance. | No | |
| 103. | C8-C9 | The student's resistance leads to a large class size. | No | |
| **104.** | **C9-C8** | **Large class size leads to the student's resistance.** | **Yes** | **The educator's attention gets neglected.** |
| **C9 Large Class Size** | | | | |
| 105. | C9-C11 | Large class size leads to lack of management awareness. | No | |
| **106.** | **C11-C9** | **Lack of management awareness leads to a large class size.** | **Yes** | **Management is not aware that the flipped class requires moderate class strength.** |
| **107.** | **C9-C10** | **Large class size leads to the educator's resistance.** | **Yes** | **Unsatisfactory course delivery** |
| 108. | C10-C9 | The educator's resistance leads to a large class size. | No | |
| **C10 Educator's Resistance** | | | | |
| 109. | C10-C11 | The educator's resistance leads to lack of management awareness. | No | |
| **110.** | **C11-C10** | **Lack of management awareness leads to the educator's resistance.** | **Yes** | **No initiatives to persuade educators** |

**Table 4.8** Reachability Matrix

| Variables | 1 | 2 | 3 | 4 | 5 | 6 | 7 | 8 | 9 | 10 | 11 |
|---|---|---|---|---|---|---|---|---|---|---|---|
| 1 | 1 | 0 | 0 | 0 | 1 | 0 | 0 | 0 | 0 | 1 | 0 |
| 2 | 1 | 1 | 1 | 1 | 1 | 1 | 1 | 0 | 1 | 1 | 0 |
| 3 | 1 | 0 | 1 | 1 | 1 | 1 | 1 | 0 | 0 | 1 | 0 |
| 4 | 0 | 0 | 0 | 1 | 1 | 0 | 0 | 0 | 0 | 1 | 0 |
| 5 | 1 | 0 | 0 | 0 | 1 | 0 | 1 | 1 | 0 | 1 | 0 |
| 6 | 1 | 0 | 0 | 0 | 1 | 1 | 0 | 0 | 0 | 1 | 0 |
| 7 | 0 | 0 | 0 | 1 | 1 | 0 | 1 | 0 | 0 | 1 | 0 |
| 8 | 0 | 0 | 0 | 0 | 0 | 0 | 0 | 1 | 0 | 1 | 0 |
| 9 | 0 | 0 | 0 | 0 | 0 | 0 | 0 | 1 | 1 | 1 | 0 |
| 10 | 0 | 0 | 0 | 0 | 0 | 0 | 0 | 0 | 0 | 1 | 0 |
| 11 | 0 | 1 | 1 | 1 | 1 | 1 | 1 | 0 | 1 | 1 | 1 |

**Table 4.9** Final Reachability Matrix (Transitivity)

| Variables | 1 | 2 | 3 | 4 | 5 | 6 | 7 | 8 | 9 | 10 | 11 |
|---|---|---|---|---|---|---|---|---|---|---|---|
| 1 | 1 | 0 | 0 | 0 | 1 | 0 | 1* | 1* | 0 | 1 | 0 |
| 2 | 1 | 1 | 1 | 1 | 1 | 1 | 1 | 1* | 1 | 1 | 0 |
| 3 | 1 | 0 | 1 | 1 | 1 | 1 | 1 | 1* | 0 | 1 | 0 |
| 4 | 1* | 0 | 0 | 1 | 1 | 0 | 1* | 1* | 0 | 1 | 0 |
| 5 | 1 | 0 | 0 | 1* | 1 | 0 | 1 | 1 | 0 | 1 | 0 |
| 6 | 1 | 0 | 0 | 0 | 1 | 1 | 1* | 1* | 0 | 1 | 0 |
| 7 | 1* | 0 | 0 | 1 | 1 | 0 | 1 | 1* | 0 | 1 | 0 |
| 8 | 0 | 0 | 0 | 0 | 0 | 0 | 0 | 1 | 0 | 1 | 0 |
| 9 | 0 | 0 | 0 | 0 | 0 | 0 | 0 | 1 | 1 | 1 | 0 |
| 10 | 0 | 0 | 0 | 0 | 0 | 0 | 0 | 0 | 0 | 1 | 0 |
| 11 | 1* | 1 | 1 | 1 | 1 | 1 | 1 | 1* | 1 | 1 | 1 |

**Table 4.10** Iteration 1

| Variables (Pi) | Reachability SetR(Pi) *(Horizontal)* | Antecedent set A (Pi) *(Vertical)* | Intersection R(Pi)^A(Pi) | Level |
|---|---|---|---|---|
| 1 | 1,5,7,8,10 | 1,2,3,4,5,6,7,11 | 1,5,7 | |
| 2 | 1,2,3,4,5,6,7,8,9,10 | 2,11 | 2 | |
| 3 | 1,3,4,5,6,7,8,10 | 2,3,11 | 3 | |
| 4 | 1,4,5,7,8,10 | 2,3,4,5,7,11 | 4,5,7 | |
| 5 | 1,4,5,7,8,10 | 1,2,3,4,5,6,7,11 | 1,4,5,7 | |
| 6 | 1,5,6,7,8,10 | 2,3,6,11 | 6 | |
| 7 | 1,4,5,7,8,10 | 1,2,3,4,5,6,7,11 | 1,4,5,7 | |
| 8 | 8,10 | 1,2,3,4,5,6,7,8,9,11 | 8 | |
| 9 | 8,9,10 | 2,9,11 | 9 | |
| 10 | 10 | 1,2,3,4,5,6,7,8,9,10,11 | 10 | I |
| 11 | 1,2,3,4,5,6,7,8,9,10,11 | 11 | 11 | |

**Table 4.11** Iteration 2

| Variables (Pi) | Reachability SetR(Pi) *(Horizontal)* | Antecedent set A (Pi) *(Vertical)* | Intersection R(Pi)^A(Pi) | Level |
|---|---|---|---|---|
| 1 | 1,5,7,8 | 1,2,3,4,5,6,7,11 | 1,5,7 | |
| 2 | 1,2,3,4,5,6,7,8,9 | 2,11 | 2 | |
| 3 | 1,3,4,5,6,7,8 | 2,3,11 | 3 | |
| 4 | 1,4,5,7,8 | 2,3,4,5,7,11 | 4,5,7 | |
| 5 | 1,4,5,7,8 | 1,2,3,4,5,6,7,11 | 1,4,5,7 | |
| 6 | 1,5,6,7,8 | 2,3,6,11 | 6 | |
| 7 | 1,4,5,7,8 | 1,2,3,4,5,6,7,11 | 1,4,5,7 | |
| 8 | 8 | 1,2,3,4,5,6,7,8,9,11 | 8 | II |
| 9 | 8,9 | 2,9,11 | 9 | |
| 11 | 1,2,3,4,5,6,7,8,9,11 | 11 | 11 | |

**Table 4.12** Iteration 3

| Variables (Pi) | Reachability SetR(Pi) *(Horizontal)* | Antecedent set A (Pi) *(Vertical)* | Intersection R(Pi)^A(Pi) | Level |
|---|---|---|---|---|
| 1 | 1,5,7 | 1,2,3,4,5,6,7,11 | 1,5,7 | III |
| 2 | 1,2,3,4,5,6,7,9 | 2,11 | 2 | |
| 3 | 1,3,4,5,6,7 | 2,3,11 | 3 | |
| 4 | 1,4,5,7 | 2,3,4,5,7,11 | 4,5,7 | |
| 5 | 1,4,5,7 | 1,2,3,4,5,6,7,11 | 1,4,5,7 | III |
| 6 | 1,5,6,7 | 2,3,6,11 | 6 | |
| 7 | 1,4,5,7 | 1,2,3,4,5,6,7,11 | 1,4,5,7 | III |
| 9 | 9 | 2,9,11 | 9 | III |
| 11 | 1,2,3,4,5,6,7,9,11 | 11 | 11 | |

**Table 4.13** Iteration 4

| Variables (Pi) | Reachability SetR(Pi) *(Horizontal)* | Antecedent set A (Pi) *(Vertical)* | Intersection R(Pi)^A(Pi) | Level |
|---|---|---|---|---|
| 2 | 2,3,4,6, | 2,11 | 2 | |
| 3 | 3,4,6 | 2,3,11 | 3 | |
| 4 | 4 | 2,3,4,7,11 | 4 | IV |
| 6 | 6 | 2,3,6,11 | 6 | IV |
| 11 | 2,3,4,6,11 | 11 | 11 | |

**Table 4.14** Iteration 5

| Variables (Pi) | Reachability SetR(Pi) *(Horizontal)* | Antecedent set A (Pi) *(Vertical)* | Intersection R(Pi)^A(Pi) | Level |
|---|---|---|---|---|
| 2 | 2,3 | 2,11 | 2 | |
| 3 | 3 | 2,3,11 | 3 | V |
| 11 | 2,3,11 | 11 | 11 | |

**Table 4.15** Iteration 6

| Variables (Pi) | Reachability SetR(Pi) *(Horizontal)* | Antecedent set A (Pi) *(Vertical)* | Intersection R(Pi)^A(Pi) | Level |
|---|---|---|---|---|
| 2 | 2 | 2,11 | 2 | VI |
| 11 | 2,11 | 11 | 11 | |

**Table 4.16** Iteration 7

| Variables (Pi) | Reachability SetR(Pi) *(Horizontal)* | Antecedent set A (Pi) *(Vertical)* | Intersection R(Pi)^A(Pi) | Level |
|---|---|---|---|---|
| **11** | 2,11 | 11 | 11 | **VII** |

**Table 4.17** Consolidated Level of Variables

| Variables (Pi) | Reachability SetR(Pi) *(Horizontal)* | Antecedent set A (Pi) *(Vertical)* | Intersection R(Pi)^A(Pi) | Level |
|---|---|---|---|---|
| **1** | 1,5,7,8,10 | 1,2,3,4,5,6,7,11 | 1,5,7 | **III** |
| **2** | 1,2,3,4,5,6,7,8,9,10 | 2,11 | 2 | **VI** |
| **3** | 1,3,4,5,6,7,8,10 | 2,3,11 | 3 | **V** |
| **4** | 1,4,5,7,8,10 | 2,3,4,5,7,11 | 4,5,7 | **IV** |
| **5** | 1,4,5,7,8,10 | 1,2,3,4,5,6,7,11 | 1,4,5,7 | **III** |
| **6** | 1,5,6,7,8,10 | 2,3,6,11 | 6 | **IV** |
| **7** | 1,4,5,7,8,10 | 1,2,3,4,5,6,7,11 | 1,4,5,7 | **III** |
| **8** | 8,10 | 1,2,3,4,5,6,7,8,9,11 | 8 | **II** |
| **9** | 8,9,10 | 2,9,11 | 9 | **III** |
| **10** | 10 | 1,2,3,4,5,6,7,8,9,10,11 | 10 | **I** |
| **11** | 1,2,3,4,5,6,7,8,9,10,11 | 11 | 11 | **VII** |

*(Note: Levels = Level is found where entire R(pi) is covered in intersection)*

## Formation of the TISM model

In this study, the TISM technique was used to model the identified 11 variables as challenges faced by the educators in applying flipped learning pedagogy for higher education. With the help of the TISM method, contextual relationships with logic have been identified among the variables, as shown in Figure 4.12. Further, following the TISM methodology, all of the variables were partitioned and allotted levels, which was discussed in detail in the previous sections.

| | C1 | C2 | C3 | C4 | C5 | C6 | C7 | C8 | C9 | C10 | C11 |
|---|---|---|---|---|---|---|---|---|---|---|---|
| C1 | | - | - | - | Skill enhancement needs time | - | - | - | - | Innovative approach needs time | - |
| C2 | Educator remain busy in other department activities | | Institute resources are allocated for department priorities | Accomplishment of department-defined goals gets associated rewards | Different inclinations | Different priorities | Completion of assigned tasks only gets appreciation | - | Department gets more revenue from more no. of students | Educators feel disoriented | - |
| C3 | Need to spend more time | - | | Necessity not felt | Need not recognized | Needs not realized | No appreciation for innovative efforts | - | - | Educators do not get motivation | - |
| C4 | - | - | - | | No motivation for skills updating | - | - | - | - | No tangible or intangible benefits for educators | - |
| C5 | Required skills need more time | - | - | - | | - | Worthy and relevant skills are appreciated | - | - | Fear of failure | - |
| C6 | Required training helps in time management | - | - | - | Unavailability of platform to hone skills | | - | - | - | Educators remains hesitant to adopt new methods | - |
| C7 | - | - | - | Interdependent | No motivation for skills improvement | - | | - | - | Dearth of motivation | - |
| C8 | - | - | - | - | - | - | - | | - | Hostile class environment | - |
| C9 | - | - | - | - | - | - | - | Educator's attention gets neglected | | Unsatisfactory course delivery | - |
| C10 | - | - | - | - | - | - | - | - | - | | - |
| C11 | - | No interest in reforming traditional teaching approach | Different priorities | Expectations of management are different | Importance of skill enhancement not recognized | Different priorities | Indifferent attitude of management | - | Management is not aware that flipped class requires moderate class strength | No initiatives to persuade educators | |

**Figure 4.12** Contextual Relationships among Challenges

As per the TISM, all of the identified variables differed in terms of their driving power and dependence as challenges for the educators in applying flipped learning as a pedagogy for higher education. The dependence and driving power of each variable was derived based on final reachability matrix (Table 9) and is shown in Table 4.18.

**Table 4.18** Driving Power & Dependence in Reachability Matrix

| Variables | 10 | 8 | 9 | 5 | 1 | 7 | 4 | 6 | 3 | 2 | 11 | Driving power |
|---|---|---|---|---|---|---|---|---|---|---|---|---|
| 10 | 1 | 0 | 0 | 0 | 0 | 0 | 0 | 0 | 0 | 0 | 0 | 1 |
| 8 | 1 | 1 | 0 | 0 | 0 | 0 | 0 | 0 | 0 | 0 | 0 | 2 |
| 9 | 1 | 1 | 1 | 0 | 0 | 0 | 0 | 0 | 0 | 0 | 0 | 3 |
| 5 | 1 | 1 | 0 | 1 | 1 | 1 | 1 | 0 | 0 | 0 | 0 | 6 |
| 1 | 1 | 1 | 0 | 1 | 1 | 1 | 0 | 0 | 0 | 0 | 0 | 5 |
| 7 | 1 | 1 | 0 | 1 | 1 | 1 | 1 | 0 | 0 | 0 | 0 | 6 |
| 4 | 1 | 1 | 0 | 1 | 1 | 1 | 1 | 0 | 0 | 0 | 0 | 6 |
| 6 | 1 | 1 | 0 | 1 | 1 | 1 | 0 | 1 | 0 | 0 | 0 | 6 |
| 3 | 1 | 1 | 0 | 1 | 1 | 1 | 1 | 1 | 1 | 0 | 0 | 8 |
| 2 | 1 | 1 | 1 | 1 | 1 | 1 | 1 | 1 | 1 | 1 | 0 | 10 |
| 11 | 1 | 1 | 1 | 1 | 1 | 1 | 1 | 1 | 1 | 1 | 1 | 11 |
| **Dependence** | 11 | 10 | 3 | 8 | 8 | 8 | 6 | 4 | 3 | 2 | 1 | |

Further, all of the challenges were grouped into four different clusters depending on their driving powers and dependence. The four different clusters are discussed as follows and graphically represented as MICMAC analysis in Figure 4.13.

Cluster I: **Autonomous Variables**: The variables that had no influence on or dependence or linkage with any other variable under study. In the present study, variable 9 (large class size) emerged as autonomous variable.

Cluster II: **Dependent Variables**: These are the variables that were highly influenced by other variables and they eventually decided the outcome or success of the model. In the present study Educator's Resistance (variable 10) emerged as the strongest dependent variable. This means that Educator's Resistance was the major challenge that decided the fate of other challenges. In order to remove this challenge of the "Educator's Resistance," other challenges needed to be addressed first. Similarly, the other dependent variables that emerged were Student's Resistance (variable 8) and Lack of Time (variable 1), which showed that "Student Resistance" and "Lack of Time" were the challenges that are highly dependent on other challenges for their improvement, but once improved they can lead to achievement of desired outcomes.

Cluster III: **Linkage Variables**: Linkage variables were the most unstable variables and little enhancement or improvement in other variables influenced them a lot. In the present study challenges, viz. Lack of Educator's Skills (variable 5), Lack of Recognition (variable 7), and Lack of Incentives (variable 4) emerged as the linkage variables. This shows that all of these challenges may be improved by giving emphasis to improving the driving variables. Further, if the challenges appearing as linkage variables are corrected, they will lead to improvement in the most dependent challenge, i.e. Educator's Resistance.

Cluster IV: **Independent Variables**: These are the strongest drivers for the other variables. They act as strategic variables and influence the model in achieving its objectives. In the present study, Lack of Management Awareness (variable 11) emerged as the most significant driving factor, followed by Inadequate Workshops/Trainings (variable 6), Lack of Institutional Support (Variable 3), and Competing Departmental goals (variable 2). This reflects that if management is aware of the benefits of flipped teaching and supports its implementation, then other challenges can also be improved. Similarly, if management begins to realize the importance of workshops and trainings to their faculty, provides all of the required institutional support, brings congruence to the department and individual goals, then this will lead to improvement of challenges in the category of the linkage variables, which will further improve the dependent variables/challenges.

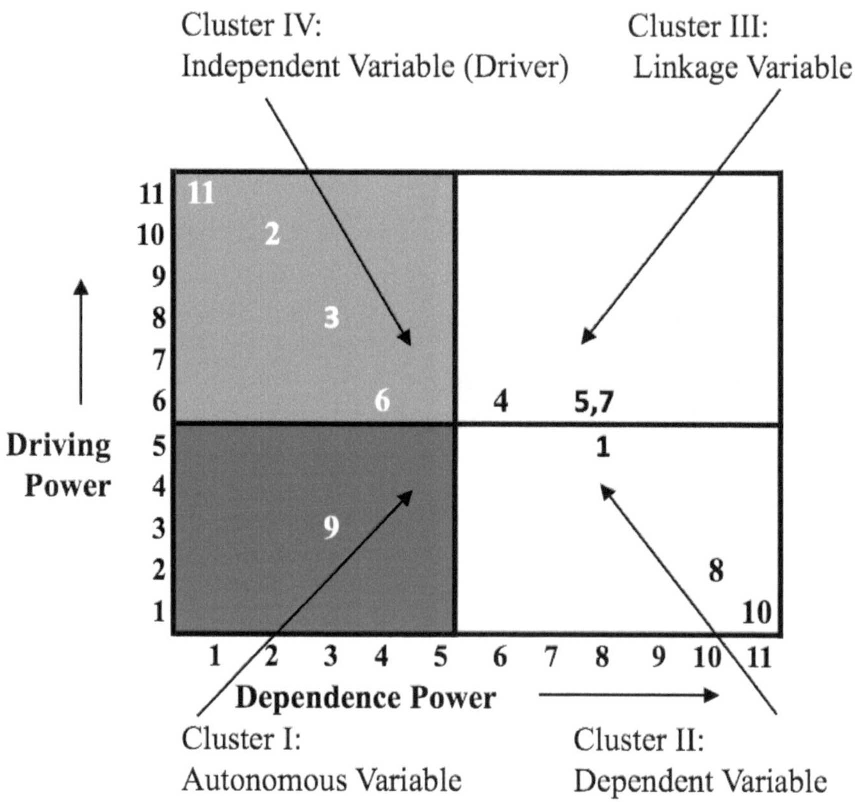


**Figure 4.13** MICMAC Analysis

## 4.4 Framework for Effective Implementation of Flipped Learning in Higher Education in India

As of now, Indian education policy does not have a comprehensive policy measure/framework for the effective implementation of the flipped learning pedagogy in institutes of higher learning in the country. The data collected through the case study of the college that has implemented flipped learning for its academic programs, interviews with educators and administrators, focus group discussions with educators from various universities in India, and the questionnaire survey were analyzed in order to identify the challenges (variables) faced by educators in adopting the flipped learning pedagogy in higher education in India, thus impacting the effective implementation of it. These challenges were modeled using the technique of Total Interpretive Structural Modeling (as described in section 4.11), and the diagraph thus created (as shown in Figure 4.8 below) with challenges placed at seven levels categorized into those having driving power and dependence, and linkage and autonomous (graphically represented as MICMAC analysis in Figure 4.6) provides the framework for the implementation of flipped learning for higher education in India.

Figure 4.14 shows the TISM-based model of the challenges that need to be addressed for successful implementation of the flipped learning pedagogy in higher education in India. The eleven challenges have been divided into seven levels, with the seventh level indicating the highest level of importance that is evident in this model. The direction of the relationship formed between this challenge of "Lack of Management Awareness" at the seventh level leads to all other challenges beginning from the sixth to the first level. Additionally, when plotted in the MICMAC matrix, "Lack of Management Awareness" also indicates the highest driving power, meaning any improvement in this variable will lead to improvement in tackling other challenges. Equally important is the challenge the "Educator's Resistance" at the first level and which in the MICMAC matrix emerged as a highly dependent variable, meaning that it is dependent on the improvement of other challenges, but once improved they can lead to the achievement of the desired outcomes.

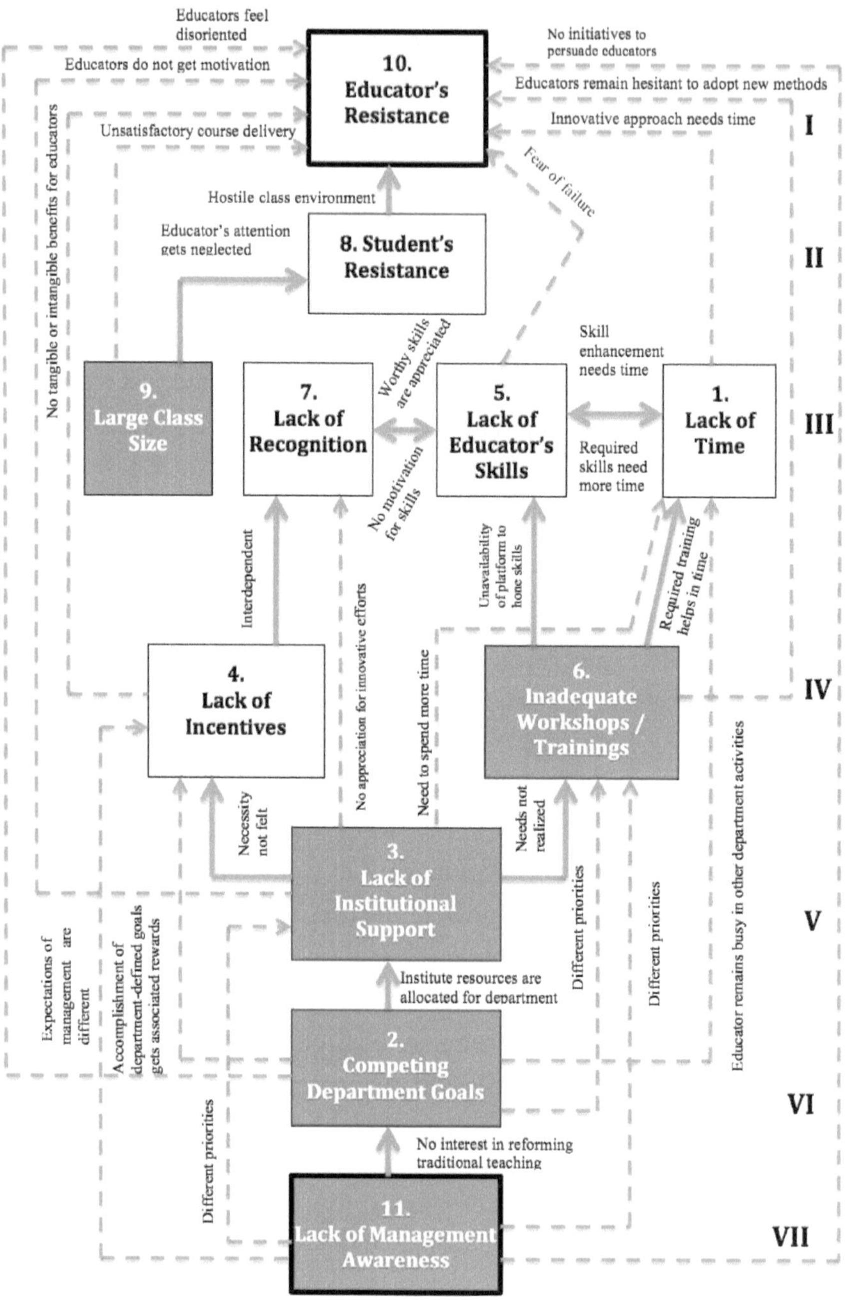

**Figure 4.14** TISM-based Model (Diagraph) for the Implementation of Flipped Learning Pedagogy in Higher Education in India

Thus, the most important factor is the management (i.e. top governing body of the institute) awareness and its willingness to implement flipped learning pedagogy at its institute. The management needs to be cognizant of the multifold benefits of flipped teaching for the learning outcomes of students and only when they accept this pedagogical approach will they take the necessary actions to materialize the adoption of flipped learning pedagogy. They need to understand that the requirement of the day is to produce graduates with an overall personality, one that can fit in a versatile job market, possessing life-long learning attitudes and capabilities, rather than just producing graduates with technical and specialized skills. This was found in the case of the private college in India that was visited for case study purposes; that unless the top management is supportive and willing to plunge into any new initiatives, it is next to impossible to implement it. None of the research papers reviewed for this study highlighted this aspect, and it was found that educators on their own had adopted the flipped learning approach as either an experiment or because they found it appropriate for their respective course. However, it is obvious from the two examples, one in India and one in Turkey, where the flipped learning approach was adopted across the institute for all of its programs offerings, that it was the will and support of the top management that made it possible to implement it successfully. Further, in response to the descriptive type question in the questionnaire survey conducted for this study, i.e. "Is there anything else that you would like to suggest regarding flipped learning or to improve the flipped classroom?" one of the respondents made a distinct suggestion: "The role of the director/principal/vice chancellor/top management of respective institutes are critical in the successful and sustainable adoption of flip pedagogy. Therefore, the training of administrators to sensitize them about the benefits of flipped learning pedagogy is a must." This again validates the model findings, that management awareness of flipped learning is most important for reaching the objective of the implementation of flipped learning in any institute.

With the strong driving power that "Lack of Management Awareness" has achieved in this model, it indicates that the top-down approach will only work in the case of India for the implementation of flipped learning pedagogy in higher education. For example in the case of the private college in India, it was the decision of the management to begin using flipped learning as their pedagogical approach, and so they recruited faculty accordingly, cautioning them that they will need to adopt a flipped classroom teaching style if recruited and that the traditional approach would not be acceptable. A top-down approach was also evident in the case of other university established as Skill University, where the vice chancellor of this university during the interview conducted for this study stated that they have recruited faculty for 2 years that have been asked to work with industries in developing curricula with internships as an important part of the curriculum structure. The management will begin offering courses only once the faculty designs the curriculum accordingly. Thus, if the management is aware and willing to implement flipped learning, the other three variables found to have driving power – in order of their significance "Competing Departmental Goals" (variable 2) at Level VI, "Lack of Institutional Support" (variable 3) at Level V, and "Inadequate Workshops/Trainings" (variable 6) at Level IV – will be accordingly addressed by the management. The departmental goals will be adjusted with flipped learning implementation being a priority, institutional support will be provided to the educators in whatever ways are needed, such as technical support both in resource form and manpower form, teaching assistants, etc., and at the same time workshops and trainings will be conducted on flipped learning internally or educators would be permitted to attend related workshops/trainings when conducted externally.

Furthermore, the awareness of management of the benefits of flipped teaching brings congruence to the department goals, leading to institutional support in the form of technical, resource, and manpower support, and supporting participation of educators in workshops and trainings. All of this then further leads to the improvement of challenges in the category of linkage variables, which as per the model are "Lack of Incentives" (variable 4), "Lack of Recognition" (variable 7), and "Lack of the Educator's Skills" (variable 5) that fall in Level IV, Level V, and Level VI in order of their significance. These linkage variables are highly unstable in the sense that any change amongst these variables affects others. In this case, if management begins to provide incentives to educators, it will feel a sense of recognition and be motivated to enhance individual skills, which in turn will make it convenient to adopt flipped learning.

The dependent variables that emerged in this study (as shown in Figure 4.7) are "Educator's Resistance" (variable 10) being most crucial at level I, followed by "Student's Resistance" (variable 8) at Level II, and "Lack of Time" (variable 1) at Level III. These are the challenges that are totally dependent on the actions taken on other challenges in the system. Thus, it is worthwhile to concentrate efforts on other challenges affecting these challenges. Unless the educator him/herself is keen to adopt the flipped teaching approach, it is impossible to implement the flipped learning pedagogy, and for this appropriate support needs to be provided in the form of technical and manpower support, incentives and recognition, and workshops/trainings to enhance their skills, providing them with adequate time by reducing their teaching load and other administrative responsibilities and allowing them to focus on preparing for the flipped classroom, which initially requires extra time and effort. Additionally, the students' resistance needs to be tackled by conveying the benefits of flipped learning pedagogy and sensitizing them about long-term impact that it will have on them by honing their all-round personality required for their selection in the job market. The ways in which all of these challenges are addressed have multifold impacts on all other challenges and this is obviously in the hands of the top management, which decides the direction and strategies for the institute.

One of the variables emerged as autonomous, which was not considered an integral part of the system and not a significant challenge, as it has no influence or dependence or linkage with any other variable.

Though in the focus group discussion, some of the faculty members cited large class sizes as one of the concerns in the adoption of flipped learning, and mentioned that it would be difficult for educators to focus on many different groups of students that would be formed for group discussion and other class activities, which is an integral part of flipped classroom teaching, it is not linked to the implementation of flipped learning pedagogy as such. Large class sizes remain a challenge even in traditional teaching approaches in the sense that individual attention cannot be given to each student. In fact, in flipped classrooms at least the students can learn from their peers and be more active learners.

## Chapter 5

# CONCLUSION

Digital pedagogy in various forms is the future of education, requiring adjustments in teaching and learning methodologies. While India has initiated digital educational schemes such as SWAYAM and e-Pathshala, it still depends and places emphasis on the traditional system of teaching by delivering lectures in class, which are mainly based on textbooks, with hardly any change in the learning outcomes and profiles of the graduates. The students need to develop life-long learning skills for the ever-changing job requirements in this fast evolving world, which requires active learning encompassing participation from both students and the educator. The Indian government does realize this and in line with the Draft National Education Policy 2019 states the following: "Instead of solely mechanistic rote learning, colleges and universities must encourage active learning to develop the abilities of independent, logical, scientific thinking, creativity, problem solving and decision-making. It must engage young people in national issues and concerns of the day" (Government of India, 2019).

Various modern approaches have evolved to induce the "so-called 21st century skills such as critical thinking, communication and collaboration, creativity, information, media and technology skills" (Bellanca & Brandt, 2010), and for this, students need to be more active learners rather than just be passive listeners in class, where the flow of information and knowledge is one-way from instructor to students, with learning that encompasses participation from both students and the educator. One such pedagogical approach that has become popular during the past decade and that extensively uses active learning methodology is flipped learning.

Traditionally it has been teachers giving lectures in class and leaving the application of knowledge entirely to students. However, this style of teaching is not effective, as one does not really know if students have really grasped the topic, as there is hardly any time left for interaction between the teacher and students. Moreover, each student has different capabilities of understanding the topic just listening to the lecture one time. Thus, it is important to provide reference material, presentations, video lectures etc., which are also easily available on the Internet, prior to the class. The class session should be devoted more to active learning rather than just one-way lecture flow. This active learning is the key to enhancing the grasping of knowledge and since students interact during class on topics through discussion amongst peers and with teachers, it stays with them without any need to memorize the topics. It also helps in developing soft skills for the students and makes them life-long learners, rather than being spoon-fed. Considering the potential that flipped learning has in enhancing the learning experience and outcomes of students, and with the education ecosystem being conducive to the use of ICT in India, the question addressed in this study concerned why educators are not adopting it.

## 5.1 Findings and Recommendations

To come up with a policy framework for flipped learning pedagogy for higher education in India, it is crucial to understand how many educators in Indian higher education institutes are aware of flipped learning and actually flip courses. A total of 297 educators' responses from more than 100 higher education institutes collected as primary data for this research study were analyzed. It was found that while 64 percent of educators are aware of flipped learning/classrooms, only 21 percent have actually flipped a course. This suggests that even with widespread awareness, issues exist in implementing flipped learning in Indian higher education. However, it is clear that flipped learning will grow further in India in the coming years as 97 percent indicated that they would like to adopt flipped learning. Thus, it is important to have policy interventions at the institute's administration level to help in this direction.

Based on the educators' responses, the experience of flipping courses was found to be overwhelmingly positive, with 57 percent of the respondents finding that flipping courses was "definitely" or "somewhat" a positive experience and 62 percent of the respondents finding it to change the way they teach now. However, preparation for using flipped learning was found to be challenging with 37 percent of the respondents responding that it was more difficult than anticipated. The willingness of the institution is probably the first step in implementing flipped learning.

Notably, only 28 percent of educators responded that their institution provided technical support and 34 percent of the educators were provided with workshops and trainings on flipped learning. Only 33 percent of the educators were provided with monetary or promotional incentives to teach a flipped learning course. Furthermore, only 35 percent of the educators had their teaching load lowered in order to encourage the preparation of other flipped courses, and this, coupled with the fact that lack of time was cited as the biggest challenge, is an important element for higher education institutions and policymakers to keep in mind. Even though professors and students have positive views of flipped learning, without institutional support, it is difficult to implement it. In fact, it is clear that institutions need to be doing more to provide workshops and trainings on flipped learning and technical support if more professors are to be willing to implement it. Without monetary or promotional incentives, this would be difficult to implement in the context of higher education, which tends to reward publishing/research more than teaching.

In the Indian context, the educators' responses were overwhelmingly positive, with 63 percent of them agreeing that flipped learning should be used across their institutions, and additionally, 67 percent believing that flipped learning is more beneficial than traditional learning. This level of optimism in flipped learning from educators was reassuring and suggests that flipped learning is highly implementable within the Indian higher education system.

The five key drivers that emerged when applying the factor analysis on the primary data were as follows:

i. Students' Improved Learning Outcome:

- Students are more collaborative in a flipped course.
- Students see the value in a flipped learning experience.
- Students build relationships/community feeling in a flipped course.
- Students are comfortable using technology for a flipped course.
- Students come to class prepared for a flipped course.
- Students adapt to the flipped learning approach.
- Students ask more questions in a flipped course.
- Students' grades are improved in a flipped course.
- Students are more engaged in a flipped course.
- Students prefer flipped courses more than the traditional approach.
- Students are not resistant to a flipped course.

ii. Institutional Support through Administrative Support and Incentives

- Manpower support is provided to encourage offering flipped learning.
- Technical support is provided to encourage offering flipped learning.
- Monetary/promotional incentives should be provided to encourage offering flipped learning.
- Workshops/trainings are conducted to encourage offering flipped learning.
- Teaching loads are reduced to allow preparing for flipped learning.

iii. Conveniences and Flexibility in Implementation

- Flipped teaching can be implemented incrementally for all programs across the institute/university.
- Flipped teaching can be implemented across the programs in the institute/university.
- Flipped teaching can be implemented as it is beneficial for students.
- Flipped teaching can be applied to selected courses only.

iv. Educators' Satisfactory Experience

- Flipped teaching is more interactive.
- Flipped courses cover more content.
- The experience of teaching a flipped course is positive.

v. Flipped Course Preparation and Delivery Convenience

- Preparing for a flipped course is convenient.
- Teaching a flipped course is convenient.

The other key findings from the interviews, case study, and focus group discussions were the following:

i. Resistance and agitation are faced by both the students and parents due to the lack of understanding of this pedagogical approach. Thus, creating awareness of flipped learning and conveying multifaceted benefits for all concerned stakeholders are important.

ii. Support would be required from the educational regulatory bodies to allow a waive-off from traditional examinations based on the students' performance evaluation. In flipped learning, the students' performance needs to be continuously evaluated.

iii. The flipped learning pedagogy should be implemented only after appropriate infrastructure vis-à-vis new classrooms, multi-media studios and smart boards, high speed Internet-enabled campuses, and other facilities are ensured.

iv. The underlying requirement for successful implementation of flipped learning pedagogy is the commitment of the management and the consistent effort of the administration and educator to ensure a supportive ecosystem.

v. The leap to flipped learning should not be made until the ecosystem is fully developed for its implementation, the classrooms have all of the necessary facilities, the campus is fully Wi-Fi enabled with high Internet speed required to download videos and lessons from anywhere, educators are well trained in using this teaching method, and so on. Thus, step-wise and incremental implementing would be suitable that allows making the necessary adjustments.

vi. The training and motivation of the educator are crucial for the success of this mode of learning/teaching, and initially educators from developing institutes/universities should be trained. The educators from the more reputed and large institutions are difficult to change, as they feel more comfortable with their traditional system of teaching.

vii. The existing courses on the national MOOCs platform "Swayam" should be utilized while also developing more video lectures that can go into this repository.

The main objective of this study was to identify challenges and how to address them in order to enable the adoption of flipped learning pedagogy by educators in higher education institutes in India. Altogether eleven challenges were identified – lack of time, competing department goals, lack of institutional support, lack of incentives, lack of the educator's skills, inadequate workshops/trainings, lack of recognition, students' resistance, large class sizes, the educator's resistance, and lack of management awareness. These challenges were modeled using the Total Interpretive Structural Modeling technique, which is very useful for qualitative study when trying to establish and build up relationships and to discover causality. The diagraph thus created (as shown in Figure 4.14) with variables (challenges) placed at seven levels categorized into those having driving power, dependence, linkages and being autonomous, provides a framework for the implementation of flipped learning for higher education in India.

Management awareness emerged as having the highest driving power to address the educator's resistance in the implementation of flipped learning pedagogy. The role of director/principal/vice chancellors/top management of respective institutes is critical in the successful and sustainable adoption of flipped learning pedagogy. Therefore, training administrators in order to sensitize them about the benefits of flipped learning pedagogy is a must. The awareness of management of the benefits of flipped teaching brings congruence to the department goals, leading to institutional support in the form of technical, resource, and manpower support, and supporting the participation of educators in workshops and trainings. If management begins to provide incentives to educators, they will feel a sense of recognition and will be motivated to enhance their individual skills, which in turn will make it convenient to adopt flipped learning. The students' resistance needs to be tackled by communicating the benefits of flipped learning pedagogy and sensitizing them about the long-term impact that it would have on them by honing their all-round personality required for their selection in the job market. Large class sizes were cited as one of the concerns in the adoption of flipped learning; however, it is not linked to the implementation of flipped learning pedagogy as such. Large class sizes remain a challenge even in a traditional teaching approach in the sense that individual attention cannot be given to each student. In fact, in flipped classrooms, at least the students can learn from their peers and be more active learners.

## 5.2 Conclusion

The implementation of flipped learning pedagogy is possible in Indian institutes of higher learning, with educators and students being receptive about it and believing that it is beneficial for students' learning outcomes with skills developed corresponding to 21$^{st}$ century needs. However, the awareness of the institute's management and its willingness is probably the first step in implementing flipped learning. Furthermore, a top-down approach will need to be applied with institutes' management taking the lead, implementing strategies and actions to achieve this aim of implementing flipped learning pedagogy in their respective institutes. Unless they are willing to provide needed support, educators on their own would be unable to adopt it due to the challenges faced, which can be addressed only with the intervention of top management and administration.

To begin with, it is recommended that instead of trying to implement flipped learning pedagogy in the top institutes of India, where educators are found to be rigid having worked in well-established education ecosystems, the strategy should be to try to implement it in the upcoming institutes/universities/colleges and to use them as models of implementation. It is comparatively easy to implement something new and innovative when institutes are in their nascent stage as they can build their policies accordingly, beginning by recruiting educators, enrolling students with information on the teaching approaches that will be used, and making them aware of it in advance in order to avoid their resistance later, building facilities needed, creating examination systems that are appropriate for flipped learning, etc.

Although the flipped learning concept seems to be simple and straightforward, it requires careful preparation, and supportive and appropriate policies. Arbitrary implementation may result in unsatisfied educators and students, which will result in its failure. Introducing flipped learning requires a lot of effort on part of educators, including priming new skills. Thus, all support and incentives must be provided in order to motivate them. However, time investment should not be looked at as merely extra work, but rather as professional quality improvement measures. The assessment of students' learning outcomes is another area that would need to be addressed, which includes continuous assessment rather than mere periodical examination per semester as in traditional teaching.

## 5.3 Policy Recommendations and Actions for Indian Higher Education Institutes

Noting that the Indian educational ecosystem is conducive to implementing flipped learning pedagogy, with educators being receptive, institute campuses being Wi-Fi enabled, and the government being supportive in terms of providing the needed facilities, the following are suggested policy recommendations and actions:

i. To implement flipped learning pedagogy, it is important to have policy intervention at the institute's management level.

ii. The institute's management awareness and its willingness are most important for successfully implementing flipped learning pedagogy.

iii. The top-down approach, where the institute's management takes the lead and implements strategies and actions, such as providing incentives in the form of monetary support and promotions, adequate training/workshops for educators, and reducing educators' other administrative workloads to be able to focus and to create spare time for developing flipped courses, is needed.

iv. It is not a condition that educators create their own video content and so the use of numerous free platforms available in India such as SWAYAM/MOOCs, E-Pathshaala etc. could be allowed and counted toward credit requirements. The educator can either create his/her own recordings to customize the course content or can create a package of already available resources.

v. Recruit educators that adapt to the flipped learning mode and are ready to use it as their pedagogical approach need to be ready to integrate active learning, student perceptions, and the use of technology in the course redesign in order to employ the flipped classroom.

vi. Government support in implementing flipped learning should be for the institutes that are upcoming or developing, especially in the states where developed institutes are lacking. Other institutes can then follow them as role models.

vii. Careful implementation by educators should be encouraged, and arbitrary implementation should be discouraged. It is important that the educator interested in flipping his/her classroom not be left to do it independently from the institutional standards or support systems.

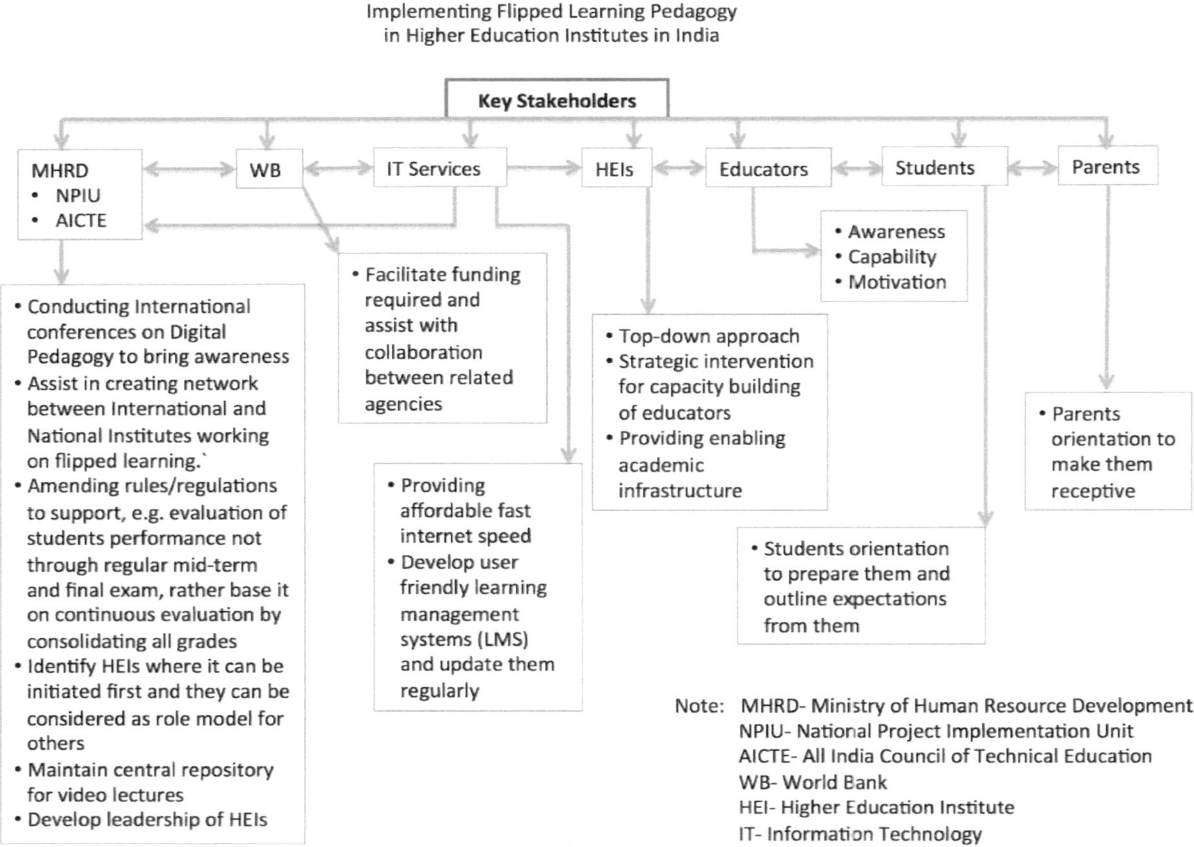


**Figure 5.1** Flipped Learning Pedagogy: A Policy Framework for Higher Education in India

## 5.4 Future Research

In this study it was found that educators in higher education institutes in India are receptive to adopting flipped learning pedagogy. However, they are unable to implement it as a pedagogical approach at the institute level on their own, and the institute's management willingness and its intervention are needed. Equally important is the support needed from the educational regulatory bodies of the government to move in this direction.

In 2002-03, the government of India with financial assistance from the World Bank launched the Technical Education Quality Improvement Program (TEQIP) as a long-term program, to be implemented in three phases for the systemic transformation of the technical education system. Under TEQIP-II and III (second and third phase) for the digital transformation of education, the Ministry of Human Resource and Development (MHRD), India had announced its support of 100 select institutions. Under this scheme, it is aimed at making the learning-teaching process interactive and popularizing flipped or blended learning as an advanced pedagogical approach, and for this educators will be trained in flipped learning pedagogy with an objective (i) to empower faculty members by upgrading their capacity (teaching abilities) to adapt digital pedagogy; (ii) to establish an active learning environment through smart classes in institutions for the students; and (iii) to enhance the employability of students while protecting their interests.

The JIS College of Engineering in India, considered as a pioneer in applying flipped learning pedagogy in its academic programs, has been assigned to conduct training workshops for educators, and it has already begun to run this in batches, beginning in November 2019. It is hoped that with this training, many educators will adopt flipped learning in their teaching.

Thus, future research areas could be (i) to see the impact of these training/workshops on educators; (ii) to identify what enabling and challenging factors are faced by the trained educators that adopt flipped learning; (iii) to see if there is any increase in the students' active participation in classrooms due to the effective use of digital pedagogy tools such as the SWAYAM/MOOCs platforms and online learning resources; (iv) to see if there is any improvement in the knowledge, skills, and behavior (KSB) of students and (v) the role of higher education institute management and regulatory bodies of India in the implementation of flipped learning pedagogy.

# BIBLIOGRAPHY


Ahmed, H. O. K. (2016). Flipped Learning As A New Educational Paradigm: An Analytical Critical Study. European Scientific Journal, ESJ, 12(10), 417. https://doi.org/10.19044/esj.2016.v12n10p417

Amutha, S., & Balakrishnan, M. (2015). Experiences and Challenges of using Flipped Classroom by Postgraduate Students: A Preliminary Comparative Study between India and Malaysia. Sian Journal of Humanities and Social Studies, 3(5), 376–381.

Angelova, N., Kiryakova, G., & Yordanova, L. (2014). Flipped Classroom–a pedagogical model for active learning. November 2017. http://dspace.uni- sz.bg/handle/123456789/72

Aronson, N., & Arfstrom, K. (2013). Flipped Learning in Higher Education. Flipped Learning Network, 1–4. http://www.flippedlearning.org/cms/lib07/VA01923112/Centricity/Domain/41/Hig herEdWhitePaper FINAL.pdf

Baker, J. W. (2000). Classroom_Flip_Baker_2000.Pdf.

Bakhru, Kanupriya M. (2013). A Principal Component Analysis of Teaching Competencies Required for Management Education. APJEM Arth Prabhand: A Journal of Economics and Management, 2(7), 1–15. https://www.researchgate.net/publication/322936153_A_Principal_Component_An alysis_of_Teaching_Competencies_Required_for_Management_Education

Bakhru, Kanupriya Misra. (2018). Aligning teaching methods for learning outcomes: A need for educational change in management education using quality function deployment approach. International Journal of Learning and Change, 10(1), 54–69. https://doi.org/10.1504/IJLC.2018.089533

Bellanca, J., & Brandt, R. (2010). 21st Century Skills: Rethinking How Students Learn.

Bloomington, IN: Solution Tree.

Bergmann, J., & Sams, A. (2014). Jonathan Bergmann and Aaron Sams.

Berrett, D. (2012). How "Flipping" the Classroom Can Improve the Traditional Lecture.

The Chronicle of Higher Education. https://www.chronicle.com/article/How- Flipping-the-Classroom/130857

Bishop, J., & Verleger, M. (2013). Testing the flipped classroom with model-eliciting activities and video lectures in a mid-level undergraduate engineering course. Proceedings - Frontiers in Education Conference, FIE, 161–163. https://doi.org/10.1109/FIE.2013.6684807

Brandt, D. S. (1997). Teaching Under. Communications of the ACM, 40(10).

Cheng, L., Ritzhaupt, A. D., & Antonenko, P. (2019). Effects of the flipped classroom instructional strategy on students' learning outcomes: a meta-analysis. In Educational Technology Research and Development (Vol. 67, Issue 4). Springer US. https://doi.org/10.1007/s11423-018-9633-7

Davies, R. S., Dean, D. L., & Ball, N. (2013). Flipping the Classroom and Instructional Technology Integration in a College-Level Information Systems Spreadsheet Course. The Learning and Technology Library, 61(4), 563–580.

de Jong, T. (2010). Cognitive load theory, educational research, and instructional design: Some food for thought. Instructional Science, 38(2), 105–134. https://doi.org/10.1007/s11251-009-9110-0

Deslauriers, L., Schelew, E., & Wieman, C. (2011). Improved learning in a large- enrollment physics class. Science, 332(6031), 862–864. https://doi.org/10.1126/science.1201783

Eppard, J., & Rochdi, A. (2017). A framework for flipped learning. Proceedings of the 13th International Conference on Mobile Learning 2017, ML 2017, 33–40.

Faculty Focus. (2015). Special Report Flipped Classroom Trends: A Survey of College Faculty Flipped Classroom Trends. Faculty Focus, August, 17. http://www.facultyfocus.com/wp-content/uploads/images/Flipped-Classroom- Trends_FF-Report-2015.pdf

Fell Kurban, C. (2015). Taking a Flipped Approach to Higher Education: Designing Universities for Today's Knowledge Economies and Societies. Academia.

Fitzpatrick, M. (2012). Classroom Lectures go Digital. New York Times. https://www.nytimes.com/2012/06/25/us/25iht-educside25.html

Flipped Learning Global Initiative. (2018). https://flglobal.org/international_definition/

Gifford, D. (2012). Flipped classroom movement gains steam. https://www.stanforddaily.com/2012/12/05/flipped-classroom-movement-gains- steam/

Gillette, C. (2018). Ac ce A pt JP ed E ft. September. https://doi.org/10.5688/ajpe7233

Gopalan, C., & Klann, M. C. (2017). The effect of flipped teaching combined with modified team-based learning on student performance in physiology. Advances in Physiology Education, 41(3), 363–367. https://doi.org/10.1152/advan.00179.2016

Government of India, M. of E. (2019). National education policy, 2019. In Ministry of Education Government of India.

Hamdam, N., McKnight, P., McKnight, K., Arfstrom, K. M., Hamdan, N., McKnight, P., McKnight, K., & Arfstrom, K. M. (2013). The Flipped Learning Model. A White Paper Based on the Literature Review Titled A Review of Flipped Learning. Arlington, VA: Flipped Learning Network 2013. LitReview_FlippedLearning1. Pdf [Viewed 24 October 2014], c.

Hao, Y. (2016). Exploring undergraduates' perspectives and flipped learning readiness in their flipped classrooms. Computers in Human Behavior, 59, 82–92. https://doi.org/10.1016/j.chb.2016.01.032

Hashemifardnia, A., Namaziandost, E., & Shafiee, S. (2018). The Effect of Implementing Flipped Classrooms on Iranian Junior High School Students' Reading Comprehension. Theory and Practice in Language Studies, 8(6), 665. https://doi.org/10.17507/tpls.0806.17

He, Y., Lu, J., Huang, H., He, S., Ma, N., Sha, Z., Sun, Y., & Li, X. (2019). The effects of flipped classrooms on undergraduate pharmaceutical marketing learning: A clustered randomized controlled study. Plos One, 14(4), 1–22. https://doi.org/10.1371/journal.pone.0214624

Howitt, C., & Pegrum, M. (2015). Implementing a flipped classroom approach in postgraduate education: An unexpected journey into pedagogical redesign. Australasian Journal of Educational Technology, 31(4), 458–469. https://doi.org/10.14742/ajet.2439

IAMAI Report. (2019).

James Bellanca and Ron Brandt. (2010). Rethinking How Students Learn. In Solution Tree Press.

Karabulut-Ilgu, A., Jaramillo Cherrez, N., & Jahren, C. T. (2018). A systematic review of research on the flipped learning method in engineering education. British Journal of Educational Technology, 49(3), 398–411. https://doi.org/10.1111/bjet.12548

Keller, B. (2011). The University of Wherever. New York Times. https://www.nytimes.com/2011/10/03/opinion/the-university-of-wherever.html

Khan, S. (2011). Let's use video to reinvent education. Khan Academy.

Kim, K.-J., & Bonk, C. (2006). The Future of Online Teaching and Learning in Higher Education: The Survey Says... EDUCAUSE Quarterly, 29(4), 22–30.

Kim, M. K., Kim, S. M., Khera, O., & Getman, J. (2014). The experience of three flipped classrooms in an urban university: An exploration of design principles. Internet and Higher Education, 22, 37–50. https://doi.org/10.1016/j.iheduc.2014.04.003

Kozikoğlu, I. (2019). Analysis of the studies concerning flipped learning model: A comparative meta-synthesis study. International Journal of Instruction, 12(1), 851– 868. https://doi.org/10.29333/iji.2019.12155a

Lakshmi, T. G., Narayana, S., Penugonda, H., Vaidya, D., Poonia, V., Ganguly, S., & Murthy, S. (2017). PIVOTeeING: A flipped approach in a postgraduate solid state devices course. Proceedings of the 25th International Conference on Computers in Education, ICCE 2017 - Main Conference Proceedings, 974–983.

Lambert, C. (2012). Twilight of the Lecture. Harvard Magazine. https://harvardmagazine.com/2012/03/twilight-of-the-lecture

Lee, J., & Choi, H. (2018). Rethinking the flipped learning pre - class : Its influence on the success of flipped learning and related factors Rethinking the flipped learning pre-class : Its influence on the success of flipped learning and related factors. April. https://doi.org/10.1111/bjet.12618

Lee, J., Lim, C., & Kim, H. (2017). Development of an instructional design model for flipped learning in higher education. Educational

Technology Research and Development, 65(2), 427–453. https://doi.org/10.1007/s11423-016-9502-1

Maycock, K. W. (2019). Chalk and talk versus flipped learning: A case study. Journal of Computer Assisted Learning, 35(1), 121–126. https://doi.org/10.1111/jcal.12317

Mayer, R. E. (2004). Should There Be a Three-Strikes Rule against Pure Discovery Learning? The Case for Guided Methods of Instruction. American Psychologist, 59(1), 14–19. https://doi.org/10.1037/0003-066X.59.1.14

Mazur, E. (2014). Peer Instruction - A user manual (Issue February).

McLaughlin, J. E., Roth, M. T., Glatt, D. M., Gharkholonarehe, N., Davidson, C. A., Griffin, L. M., Esserman, D. A., & Mumper, R. J. (2014). The flipped classroom: A course redesign to foster learning and engagement in a health professions school. Academic Medicine, 89(2), 236–243. https://doi.org/10.1097/ACM.0000000000000086

McNeill, A. K., & Bardsley, K. L. (2016). Teachers' Pedagogical Design Capacity for Scientific Argumentation. Science Education, 100(4), 645–672. https://doi.org/10.1002/sce.21222

Moravec, M., Williams, A., Aguilar-Roca, N., & K. O'Dowd, D. (2010). Learn before Lecture: A Strategy That Improves Learning Outcomes in a Large Introductory Biology Class. CBE-Life Sciences Education, 9, 473–481.

Mukherjee, M. (2017, September 7). Engineering explores "Flip" side of study. The Telegraph - Online Edition. https://www.telegraphindia.com/states/west- bengal/engineering-explores-flip-side-of-study/cid/1406630

Murray, D., Koziniec, T., & McGill, T. (2015). Student perceptions of flipped learning. Conferences in Research and Practice in Information Technology Series, 160(January), 57–62.

O'Flaherty, J., & Phillips, C. (2015). The use of flipped classrooms in higher education: A scoping review. Internet and Higher Education, 25, 85–95. https://doi.org/10.1016/j.iheduc.2015.02.002

Ozturk, I. (2001). The role of education in economic development : A theoretical framework. Journal of Rural Development and Administration, XXXIII(Winter 2001), 39–47.

Peterson, M. J. (2009). General Assembly. In The Oxford Handbook on the United Nations. https://doi.org/10.1093/oxfordhb/9780199560103.003.0005

Pierce, R., & Fox, J. (2012). Vodcasts and active-learning exercises in a "flipped classroom" model of a renal pharmacotherapy module. American Journal of Pharmaceutical Education, 76(10). https://doi.org/10.5688/ajpe7610196

Ram, M. P., & Sinha, A. (2017). An implementation framework for flipped classrooms in higher education. ACM International Conference Proceeding Series, Part F1276, 18–26. https://doi.org/10.1145/3055219.3055224

Raman, S. (2016). Emerging Trends in Higher Education Pedagogy.

Ramirez, D., Hinojosa, C., & Rodriguez, F. (2014). Advantages and Disadvantages of Flipped Classroom: Stem Students' Perceptions. Iceri 2014: 7Th International Conference of Education, Research and Innovation, May, 121–127. https://doi.org/10.13140/RG.2.1.2430.8965

Rosenberg, T. (2013). Turning Education Upside Down. https://opinionator.blogs.nytimes.com/2013/10/09/turning-education-upside-down/

Sale, D., & Cheah, S.-M. (2017). Pedagogy for Evidence-Based Flipped Classroom - Part1: Framework. 13th International CDIO Conference, At Calgary, Canada, June. https://www.researchgate.net/

publication/317993427_Pedagogy_for_Evidence- Based_Flipped_Classroom_-_Part_1_Framework

Sams, A., & Washington, O. (2012). Jonathan Bergmann.

Serin, H., & Khabibullin, A. (2019). Flipped Classrooms in Teaching Method Courses at Universities. International Journal of Academic Research in Business and Social Sciences, 9(1), 573–585. https://doi.org/10.6007/ijarbss/v9-i1/5459

Shimamoto, D. (2012). Implementing a flipped classroom: An instructional module. TCC Conference, 9. http://scholarspace.manoa.hawaii.edu/handle/10125/22527

Shnai, I. (2017). Systematic review of challenges and gaps in flipped classroom implementation : Toward future model enhancement. Proceedings of the 16th European Conference on ELearning, November, 484–490.

Stone, B. B. (2012). No Title. Proceedings from 28th Annual Conference on Distance Teaching & Learning, Madison, Wisconsin, USA.

Strayer, J. (2007). The Learning Environment : A Comparison of. Dissertation. Strayer, J. F. (2012). How learning in an inverted classroom influences cooperation,

innovation and task orientation. Learning Environments Research, 15(2), 171–193. https://doi.org/10.1007/s10984-012-9108-4

Talbert, R. (2014). Inverting the Linear Algebra Classroom. Primus, 24(5), 361–374. https://doi.org/10.1080/10511970.2014.883457

Tenneson, M. (2006). The Classroom Flip.

The World's First "Flipped Learning" University to Host Global Standards Summit. (2018). Academy of Active Learning Arts and Sciences. https://www.prnewswire.com/news-releases/the-worlds-first-flipped-learning- university-to-host-global-standards-summit-300743252.html

TOI-Online. (2018, March 6). Unemployment Rate in India. Times of India. https://timesofindia.indiatimes.com/home/education/news/unemployment-rate-in- india-nearly-31-million-indians-are-jobless/articleshow/63182015.cms

Tomas, L., Evans, N. (Snowy), Doyle, T., & Skamp, K. (2019). Are first year students ready for a flipped classroom? A case for a flipped learning continuum.

International Journal of Educational Technology in Higher Education, 16(1). https://doi.org/10.1186/s41239-019-0135-4

Zhan, Z., & Mei, H. (2013). Academic self-concept and social presence in face-to-face and online learning: Perceptions and effects on students' learning achievement and satisfaction across environments. Computers and Education, 69, 131–138. https://doi.org/10.1016/j.compedu.2013.07.002

# APPENDIX-A

Prof.Worsak Kanok Nukulchai
President

Postal Address:
P.O. Box 4, Klong Luang
Pathumthani 12120
Thailand

Street Address:
Km. 42 Paholyothin Highway
Klong Luang, Pathumthani 12120
Thailand

(For local calls, dial 02 before the tel/fax nos.)
Tel : (66-2) 524-6319 / 6001
Fax : (66-2) 524-8000
http://www.ait.asia

19th April 2018

**To Whom It May Concern**

Ms. Namita Sravat is the employee of the Asian Institute of Technology, Thailand since 1998. She currently holds the position of the Academic Affairs Officer.

Ms. Namita has been pursuing her doctoral studies at the National Institute of Development Administration, Thailand as a part-time student since August, 2014. After successfully completing her Coursework and Qualifying Exam, she is now working on her dissertation.

Following the workshop conducted on Flipped Learning by the Principal of JIS College of Engineering, Dr. Malay R Dave, Ms. Namita is keen to do her dissertation on Flipped Learning as the new pedagogical methodology, in which the JIS College of Engineering is one of the pioneer colleges in India.

In relation to Ms. Namita's dissertation work on Flipped Learning, she would like to collect questionnaire survey based data from your current students and may also need to conduct some individual interviews with faculty and administrators at the JIS College of Engineering.

Thank You.

Prof. Worsak Kanok-Nukulchai
President
Asian Institute of Technology

# APPENDIX-B

Dear Participant:

My name is Namita Sravat and I am pursuing my doctoral studies at National Institute of Development Administration (NIDA), Thailand, while also working as Academic Affairs Officer at the Asian Institute of Technology (AIT), Thailand.

For my dissertation, I am examining use of 'Flipped Learning Pedagogy' in Higher Education, specifically in undergraduate programs of universities/colleges in India. As a faculty member at one of the prestigious universities/colleges in India, I am inviting you to participate in this research study by completing the attached survey.

The following questionnaire will require approximately 15-20 minutes to complete it online on the google link https://docs.google.com/forms/d/e/1FAIpQLSfMVka823X83v4Nh_RIv9O3rLwLQQzMSbICNfHL_u0SXf8mIA/viewform?usp=sf_link

After filling first section with basic questions about yourself, please review the brief introduction on Flipped Learning to ensure that it is understood in the context of this study (Flipped Learning is at times misunderstood as online, blended or active learning). This is embedded as Section A of the Questionnaire.

I do understand that your time is valuable, but your participation in this research that is very much related to your own esteemed profession will be highly appreciated. I would thus humbly request you to answer all questions and fill it online soonest possible, but not later than 24 December 2019. Please be ensured that all the information will remain highly confidential and the data collected will be used for this dissertation work only.

The copy of this study's summary or papers published based on this study, will be shared with those who wish so by indicating it in the questionnaire. Completion of the questionnaire will indicate your willingness to participate in this study. If you require additional information or have questions, you may kindly contact me through return email.

Thank you once again for your time and support.

Yours Sincerely,

Ms. Namita Sravat
namita@ait.ac.th

Doctoral Student, Graduate School of Public Administration
National Institute of Development Administration, Thailand

Academic Affairs Officer,
President's Office, Asian Institute of Technology, Thailand

# APPENDIX-C

Date: 9 November 2019

**Subject: Focus Group Discussion**

Dear Participant:

My name is Namita Sravat and I am pursuing my doctoral studies at National Institute of Development Administration (NIDA), Thailand, while also working as Academic Affairs Officer at the Asian Institute of Technology (AIT), Thailand.

For my dissertation, I am examining use of 'Flipped Learning Pedagogy' in Higher Education, specifically in undergraduate programs of universities/colleges in India. Because you are a faculty member at one of the prestigious universities/colleges in India, I would like to invite you to participate in Focus Group Discussion that will be held on 16 November 2019 at 3:30 p.m. at Lobby Lounge, AIT Conference Center, Thailand. Following the formal discussion, we would continue discussion over tea informally.

As clarified on phone, for participating in this discussion it is not mandatory that you are experienced in teaching using Flipped Learning approach. It is more to understand that if it is not being adopted then what may be the challenges/issues involved that are faced by educators of higher education in India, and what policy interventions may be needed.

I do understand that your time is valuable, but your participation in this research that is very much related to your own esteemed profession will be highly appreciated.

Thank you in advance for accepting to participate in this discussion and providing your valuable inputs. Looking forward to see you all soon

Sincerely,

Ms. Namita Sravat

Doctoral Student,
Graduate School of Public Administration, National Institute of Development Administration, Thailand

Academic Affairs Officer,
President's Office, Asian Institute of Technology, Thailand

namita@ait.ac.th

# APPENDIX-D

## Flipped Learning Pedagogy in Higher Education, India

Questionnaire Survey for Faculty Teaching in Higher Education

* Required

1. Email address *

2. Name of Institute, Place *

3. Name: *

4. Title *

   *Mark only one oval.*

   - Lecturer
   - Assistant Professor
   - Associate Professor
   - Full Professor
   - Adjunct/Affiliated/Visiting

5. Area of Study *

6. Gender *

*Mark only one oval.*

- Male
- Female
- Prefer not to say

7. Age *

*Mark only one oval.*

- <29
- 30-39
- 40-49
- 50-59
- >60

8. Teaching at (select the highest level you teach): *

*Mark only one oval.*

- Bachelors Level
- Masters Level
- Doctoral Level
- Other: ____________

9. Teaching Experience (number of years) *

____________

10. Are you aware about Flipped Learning or Classroom *

*Mark only one oval.*

- Yes
- No
- May be

11. Which definition aligns to your interpretation of Flipped learning? *

*Mark only one oval.*

- Students complete pre-class work individually before class and engage in teamwork and collaborative learning activities during class
- Lectures are recorded as videos for students to view outside of class time freeing up time in class to engage in discussions and problem solving
- The learning environment is designed to switch the focus away from the instructor and toward the students
- The homework and lectures are reversed. Recorded lectures are viewed outside of class time, and homework is completed during class time
- Elements of all definitions above

12. Any other interpretation of your definition (Pls. specify) *

Section A - Please read the 'Overview of Flipped Learning' before proceeding

NOTE: Reading this section before proceeding to fill rest of the questionnaire is important to ensure that Flipped Learning is understood in the context of this study

## OVERVIEW OF FLIPPED LEARNING

### What is Flipped Learning?

*As per the definition composed by the governing board and key leaders of the Flipped Learning Network (FLN), "Flipped Learning is a pedagogical approach in which direct instruction moves from the group learning space to the individual learning space, and the resulting group space is transformed into a dynamic, interactive learning environment where the educator guides students as they apply concepts and engage creatively in the subject matter."*

In simple words, the traditional lecture delivery in classroom and related assignment/projects/group discussion outside classroom is flipped. The lectures are provided to students prior to class, and assignments, projects and group discussions are held inside the classroom in presence of the teacher with his guidance.

Lectures could be in form of materials such as course videos and articles prepared by academics, Excel files, PDFs, images, videos and PowerPoint slides made available to students online prior to class.

The Flipped Learning system fits seamlessly with the Bloom Taxonomy, enabling students to perform lower-level cognitive tasks such as learning and understanding earlier, and focusing on higher-level cognitive tasks such as support from peers and academics during the course and practice, analysis, synthesis and evaluation.

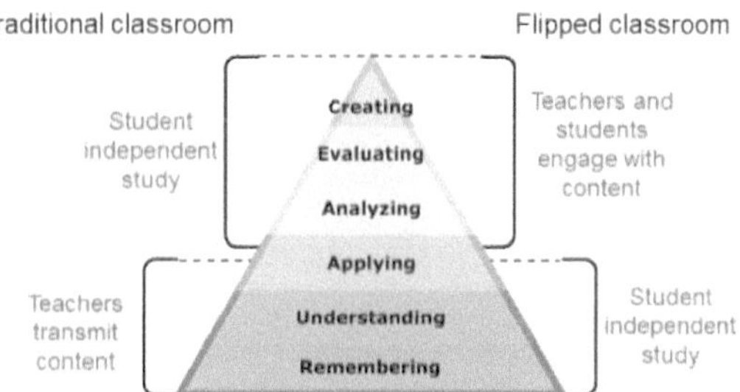


### How Learning Happens in Flipped Learning?

- Before the class, student watches the lecture video at a desired time, takes notes and enlist questions for parts not understood.
- Students transmit their questions in electronic form to the lecturer.
- The lecturer may group the students according to the nature of the questions.
- Students try to find answers to their questions in group work. The lecturer visits the groups and enables in finding answers when they cant.
- The lecturer can ask questions to test whether the students have learned the concept and can also assign group work on the problems to cover their applications.
- Active participation is there from all students in this learning.

| Advantages | Disadvantages |
|---|---|
| • Students take ownership for learning<br>• Lessons and contents are accessible anytime<br>• Promotes student-centered learning<br>• Encourages critical thinking<br>• Strengthens teamwork and co-operative skills<br>• Efficient allowing more time to explore the topic<br>• Continuous evaluation of student learning rather than waiting for mid-term or final exam results | • Creates digital divide<br>• Depends on preparation and trust<br>• Teachers will have extra work<br>• Work load for students too increases. |

## Section B - Experience of Flipped Learning

13. Have you flipped course(s)? (If "No" then move to next Section-C) *

*Mark only one oval.*

- ( ) Yes
- ( ) No

14. Since which Year have you flipped course(s)?

15. How many times have you flipped course?

16. What was the number of student in your flipped classes (average range)?

17. What were the course(s) flipped?

18. At what level the course(s) were flipped?

*Check all that apply.*

- [ ] Doctoral
- [ ] Master
- [ ] Bachelor

Other: [ ]

19. Your Experience of flipping the course(s)

*Mark only one oval per row.*

| | Definitely Not | Not Really | Can't say | Somewhat | Definitel |
|---|---|---|---|---|---|
| Was the experience of flipping the course positive? | ◯ | ◯ | ◯ | ◯ | ◯ |
| Was teaching flipped course more difficult than you anticipated? | ◯ | ◯ | ◯ | ◯ | ◯ |
| Was preparing flipped course more difficulty than anticipated? | ◯ | ◯ | ◯ | ◯ | ◯ |
| Were you able to teach and cover more course content? | ◯ | ◯ | ◯ | ◯ | ◯ |
| Has it changed the way you teach now? | ◯ | ◯ | ◯ | ◯ | ◯ |

Section C

20. Do you intend to Flip course in future *

*Mark only one oval.*

◯ Yes

◯ Maybe

◯ No

21. From your experience/perception, to what extent do you disagree/agree with following in relation to students *

*Mark only one oval per row.*

| | Strongly Disagree | Disagree | Neither | Agree | Strongly Agree |
|---|---|---|---|---|---|
| They are more engaged in class | | | | | |
| Their Grades are improved | | | | | |
| They are not resistant | | | | | |
| They prefer it over traditional approach | | | | | |
| They adapt to the approach | | | | | |
| They ask more questions | | | | | |
| They come to class prepared | | | | | |
| They are more collaborative | | | | | |
| They see value of this type of experience | | | | | |
| They are comfortable using technology | | | | | |
| They build relationships/community feeling | | | | | |

22. Does your institute/administration encourage you to offer flipped learning by doing: *

*Mark only one oval per row.*

| | Yes | No |
|---|---|---|
| Workshops/Trainings on Flipped Learning | | |
| Provides technical support | | |
| Provides manpower support | | |
| Monetary/Promotion incentive | | |
| Allows less teaching load so that other flipped course can be prepared | | |

23. What as per your experience/perception are the biggest benefits of Flipped Learning? (Check all the applies) *

*Check all that apply.*

- [ ] Increased student engagement
- [ ] Improved student learning
- [ ] Learner-centered teaching
- [ ] Improved course delivery and in re-energized course
- [ ] Helps in teaching more course content/concept in effective way
- [ ] Teacher knows student better and so can help them better with their learning
- [ ] Increased job satisfaction of teaching students effectively
- [ ] Teachers will collaborate to prepare good lectures
- [ ] All of the above
- [ ] I did not realize any tangible benefits

Other: [ ]

24. If you do not intend to flip course, then check the reasons that apply *

*Check all that apply.*

- [ ] Do not know enough on how to do it
- [ ] Not techno-savvy to do it
- [ ] Lack of recognition and/or support
- [ ] Too time consuming and limited time to prepare flipped course
- [ ] Too expensive
- [ ] Demanding and challenging
- [ ] Requires over vigilance of students in class
- [ ] Extra work load for students too
- [ ] It is just a fad, as if its new kind of pedagogy, while flipped learning has always been there in som form or other.
- [ ] Already using it in some way without using the term 'Flip'

Other: [ ]

25. 4. What challenges will be faced if you have to adopt flipping the courses? *

*Mark only one oval per row.*

| | Insignificant (Rarely a challenge) | Moderate ( Sometimes a challenge) | Can't Say | Significant (Often a challenge | Very Significant (Always a challenge) |
|---|---|---|---|---|---|
| Time | ⬭ | ⬭ | ⬭ | ⬭ | ⬭ |
| Lack of Support (resources/funding/space) | ⬭ | ⬭ | ⬭ | ⬭ | ⬭ |
| Competing department/college/campus goals | ⬭ | ⬭ | ⬭ | ⬭ | ⬭ |
| Not valued by colleagues/administration | ⬭ | ⬭ | ⬭ | ⬭ | ⬭ |
| Not understood by colleagues/administration | ⬭ | ⬭ | ⬭ | ⬭ | ⬭ |
| Being creative/developing new strategies and ideas | ⬭ | ⬭ | ⬭ | ⬭ | ⬭ |
| Student resistance/lack of motivation | ⬭ | ⬭ | ⬭ | ⬭ | ⬭ |
| My experience/comfort with technology | ⬭ | ⬭ | ⬭ | ⬭ | ⬭ |
| Other responsibilities required by my position | ⬭ | ⬭ | ⬭ | ⬭ | ⬭ |

26. 7. What would be your preferred tools/resources for use in flipped teaching? *

*Check all that apply.*

- ☐ Softwares such as Moodle, Google Classroom, Quizlet, Camstasia and other open source tools
- ☐ Lecture Videos
- ☐ Power Point Presentations
- ☐ Lecture Notes and Handouts
- ☐ Project Work, Group Discussion, Group Work, Quiz, Games and other Class Activities
- ☐ MOOCs
- ☐ Digital Libraries

Other: ☐

27. In context of India: *

*Mark only one oval per row.*

| | Strongly Disagree | Disagree | Neutral | Agree | Strongly Agree |
|---|---|---|---|---|---|
| Flipped learning would prove more beneficial for students than traditional teaching | ◯ | ◯ | ◯ | ◯ | ◯ |
| Flipped teaching should be used across the institute | ◯ | ◯ | ◯ | ◯ | ◯ |
| Initially flipped teaching should be used only for selected courses | ◯ | ◯ | ◯ | ◯ | ◯ |
| Incremental adoption of flipped teaching across the institute within stipulated time-frame | ◯ | ◯ | ◯ | ◯ | ◯ |

28. What kind of support would one need if this teaching method is to be used across the institute level in India? *

29. Do you think that flipped learning needs to be supported at government level? Can you suggest the kind of policy framework that should be there? *

30. Anything else that you would like to suggest regarding Flipped Learning or to improve flipped classroom. *

31. Please indicate below if you need copy of summary any publication from this study

*Mark only one oval.*

- ( ) Yes
- ( ) No

# APPENDIX-E

**Name of Institute, Place**

1. ABV-IIITM, Gwalior, Mathya Pradesh
2. Agro Economic Research Centre, Jorhat, Assam
3. APPAIET, Kalaburagi, Karnataka
4. Assam University, Diphu, Assam
5. Ballari Institute of Technology and management, Ballari, Karnataka
6. Bhartiya Vidya Bhawan, New Delhi
7. BIT Sindri, Dhanbad, Jharkhand
8. CAU, Imphal, Manipur
9. CBIT, Hyderabad, Telangana
10. CCS HAU, Hisar, Haryana
11. CDLU, Sirsa, Haryana
12. CMR Technical Campus, Hyderabad, Telangana
13. Colleg of Engineering, Nanded, Maharashtra
14. College Of Agricultural Engineering And Post Harvest Technology, CAU, Manipur
15. College of Horticulture and Forestry, CAU Pasighat, Arunachal Pradesh
16. College of Horticulture, Thenzawl, Mizoram
17. College of Post Graduate Studies in Agricultural Sciences, CAU, Meghalaya, Assam
18. DAIMSR, Nagpur, Maharashtra
19. Datta Meghe Institute of Management Studies, Nagpur, Maharashtra
20. Datta Meghe Institute of Management Studies, Nagpur, Maharashtra
21. DCRUST, Murtha, Haryana
22. Delhi School of Business, New Delhi
23. Delhi Technological University, New Delhi
24. DES's Navinchandra Mehta Institute of Technology and Development, Mumbai, Maharashtra
25. Dhanwate National College Congress Nagar, Nagpur, Maharashtra
26. Diploma in Fisheries Engineering, RMIT, Punjab
27. DMS, Nabira Mahavidyalaya, Katol, Maharashtra
28. Dr. Ambedkar Institute of Management Studies & Research, Nagpur, Maharashtra
29. Dr. B. R. Ambedkar National Institute of Technology Jalandhar, Punjab
30. Dr. Panjabrao Deshmukh Krishi Vidyapeeth, Akola, Maharashtra
31. Footwear Design & Development Institute, Chhindwara, Madhya Pradesh
32. GBPUAT, Pantnagar, Uttrakhand
33. G. H. Raisoni College of Engineering, Nagpur, Maharashtra
34. GCW Bawani khera, Haryana
35. GJU, Hisar, Haryana
36. Godavari Institute of Engineering and Technology Rajahmundry, Andra Pradesh
37. Godutai Engineering College for Women, Kalaburagi, Karnataka
38. Gondwana University, Gadchiroli, Maharahstra
39. Govindrao Wanjari College Of Engineering And Technology, Nagpur, Maharashtra
40. Govt Polytechnic Sirsa Haryana State Board Of Technical Education, Panchkula, Haryana

41. Govt. College, Hisar, Haryana
42. Great lakes Institute of Mgmt. Gurugram, Haryana
43. Guru Nanak Dev Engineering College, Bidar, Karnataka
44. GVRK Acharyulu, Univ. of Hyderabad, Telangana
45. Haryana Agricultural University, Hisar, Haryana
46. HBTU, Kanpur, Uttar Pradesh
47. HCST, Jamaalpur, Uttar Pradesh
48. Hyderabad Institute of Technology and Management, Hyderabad, Telanganaa
49. ICAR-NDRI, Karnal, Haryana
50. IIT (BHU), Varanasi
51. IIT, Bombay, Maharashtra
52. IIT, Delhi, New Delhi
53. IIT, Gandhinagar, Gujarat
54. IIT, Guwahati, Assam
55. IIT, Kharagpur, West Bengal
56. IIT, Madras, Tamil Nadu
57. IIT, Mandi, Himachal Pradesh
58. IIT, Roorkee, Uttrakhand
59. IMCOST, Mumbai, Maharashtra
60. Institute of Agri Business Management, SKRAU, Bikaner, Rajasthan
61. Institute of Management Technology, Ghaziabad, Uttar Pradesh
62. J C Bose University of Science and Technology, YMCA, Faridabad, Haryana
63. J D College of Engineering and Management, Nagpur, Maharashtra
64. JIT Nagpur, Maharashtra
65. JSS Noida, Uttar Pradesh
66. K J Somaiya Institute of Management Studies and Research, Mumbai, Maharashtra
67. Kamla Nehru Mahavidyalaya Nagpur, Maharashtra
68. KL University, Vaddeswaram, Guntur, Andhra Pradesh
69. KLEF, Vijaywada, Andra Pradesh
70. Kurukshetra University, Kurukshetra, Haryana
71. M B Patel College, Sakoli Dist. Bhandara, Maharashtra
72. Maharana Pratap University of Agriculture& Technology, Udaipur Rajasthan
73. Mahatma Phule Krishi Vidyapeeth, Rahuri, Maharashtra
74. Maulana Azad National Institute of Technology, Bhopal, Madhya Pradesh
75. MBM Engineering College, Jai Narain Vyas University, Jodhpur, Rajasthan
76. Mizoram University, Mizoram
77. MNNIT Allahabad, Uttar Pradesh
78. MPUAT, Udaipur, Rajasthan
79. MSG-SGKM College of Arts, Science and Commerce, Mumbai, Maharashtra
80. MSIT, Janakpuri, New Delhi
81. Nalla Narasimha Reddy Education Society's Group of Institutions Hyderabad, Telangana
82. National Institute of Construction Management and Research (NICMAR), Delhi NCR
83. National Institute of food Technology Entrepreneurship & management, Kundli, Haryana
84. National Institute of Industrial Engineering (NITIE), Mumbai, Maharashtra

85. National Institute of Technology, Warangal, Telangana
86. NIFT, Delhi, New Delhi
87. NIFT, Jodhpur, Rajasthan
88. NIFT, Gandhinagar, Gujarat
89. NIFTEM, Sonipat, Haryana
90. NIT, Patna, Bihar
91. NIT, Trichy, Tamil Nadu
92. NMIMS, Mumbai, Maharashtra
93. North Eastern Hill University, Shillong, Meghalaya
94. P D A College of Engineering, Kalaburagi, Karnataka
95. P. R. Patil Institute of Pharmacy Talegaon, Tq. Ashton, Dist. Wardha, Maharashtra
96. Punjab University, Chandigarh, Punjab
97. PDA Engineering College, Gulbarga, Karnataka
98. PDIMTR, Nagpur, Maharashtra
99. PDIT, Hospet, Karnataka
100. Poojya Doddappa Appa College of Engineering, Kalaburagi, Karnataka
101. Priyadarshini LTIMSR, Nagpur, Maharashtra
102. PTU, Punjab
103. R.B.S Engineering Technical Campus, Bichpuri, Agra
104. R.B.S Polytechnic, Bichpuri, Agra
105. Raj Kumar Goel Institute of Technology, Ghaziabad, Uttar Pradesh
106. Rashtriya Chemicals and Fertilizers Limited, Rajasthan
107. RBS SIET, Rewari, Rajasthan
108. RGKUT, Basar, Hyderabad
109. S G Balekundri Institute of Technology, Belgaum, Karnataka
110. S K Rajasthan Agricultural University, Bikaner, Rajasthan
111. S. V. National Institute of Technology Surat, Gujarat
112. Sant Longowal Ins of Engg and Tech, Sangrur, Punjab
113. SDM College of Engineering and Technology, Dharwad, Karnataka
114. Seth Kesarimal Porwal College, Kamptee, Maharashtra
115. Sharnbasva University, Kalaburagi, Karnataka
116. Shiv Nadar University, Greater Noida, Uttar Pradesh
117. SIBM, Nagpur, Maharashtra
118. SK RAU, Bikaner, Rajasthan
119. Srinivasa Ramanujan Institite of Technology, Anantapur, Andra Pradesh
120. STJIT, Ranebennur, Karnataka
121. SVCET, Chittoor, Andra Pradesh
122. SVP University of Agriculture and Technology, Meerut, Uttar Pradesh
123. The NorthCap University, Gurgaon, Haryana
124. TIET, Patiala, Punjab
125. Tolani College of Commerce, Maharashtra
126. Veerappa Nisty Engineering College, Shorapur, Maharashtra
127. VIPS, Delhi School of Business, Delhi, New Delhi

# APPENDIX-F

## TECHNOLOGICAL INFRASTRUCTURE

- When all courses need to be embedded in an institutional wide LMS (learning Management system), it is imperative to choose a secure, easy to use, closed system that allows for easy course design and course access.
- The checklist for choice of LMS includes:
- 1. Well established
- 2.Secure
- 3. User friendly
- 4. Inclusion of communication channels
- 5. Ability to track learning outcomes
- We have selected Blackboard as our best LMS option.

# THE TEAM- TEAM MEMBERS INVOLVED IN CREATING A BEST PRACTICE FLIPPED LEARNING COURSE

- **Course Development Head:**
  He is a subject matter expert, and ensures course development is in line with curricula/program goals and also ensures academic quality exists
- **Course Developer:**
  He is also a subject matter expert. He works in collaboration with the CDH to select and design course materials.
- **Instructional Designer (ID):**
  The instructional Designer works as a pedagogy and design consultant, employs the institutional Flipped Learning Instructional Design model, assists the team to selec tcourse materials and learning outcomes that support the institutional Flipped Learning pedagogical foundations, and ensures course design adheres to the institutional Flipped Learning Vision Statement and Quality Assurance parameters
- **Instructional Technologies Coordinator (ITC):**
  The ITC acts as technical support on course development projects, provides technical assistance with aspects of the technological design of the course (eg: uploading course content, designing the course banner, assisting with the look and feel of the course, assisting in importing quiz/exam questions), helps Course Developers ensure that the technologies chosen are appropriate, tests the course links, and manages the courses in the institution.
- **Recording & Post-production Team:**
  Flipped Learning needs a studio to record both the instructor as well as students interpretation of the topic that forms integral part of the digital contents. The recording and post-production team provides support in filming, editing, adding closed captions, adding backgrounds etc.
- **Library Director:**
  He reviews courses to check they are in adherence to copyright laws.

# FORMAT FOR EVALUATING THE STUDENTS GRADING: A TO F

- Digital Content - Overall
- Flow of Digital Content
- Quality/Quantity of Digital Content
- Understanding of the Digital Content
- Balance of Digital Content – A balanced mix of VDOs, animation, slide shows, flowcharts etc.
- Group Discussions
- Team work - Negotiation Skills, Respect, Passion, Commitment, Collaboration
- Leadership Qualities – Decision Making, Empathy, Awareness, Flexibility, Learning, Communication
- Attitude – Interest in Preparing the Digital Content
- Aptitude – Subject/Topic Knowledge

# EVALUATION FRAMEWORK

Credit Systems (10 –scale):

A -10 (marks 90 and >
B– 9 (80-89)
C- 8 (70-79), D- 7(60 -69),
E- 6 (40 -59),
F -2 (below 40).

## Daily evaluation sample (paper code)

| Sl no | Name of the students | University Roll No. | Digital Content -overall | Flow of Digital content | Quality of Digital content | Understanding of digital content | Balance of digital content -mix | Group Discussion | Negotiation skills | Leadership qualities | Attitude -Interest in preparing | Aptitude – subject/ topic knowledge |
|---|---|---|---|---|---|---|---|---|---|---|---|---|
| 1 | X.Y | JISCE/2017/001 | A | B | C | A | A | B | B | C | B | D |

Daily evaluation value (as above) = (10+9+8+10+10+9+9+8+9+7)/100 = 89/100 (=8.9/10)

# EVALUATION FRAMEWORK

## Evaluation Framework

### Weekly Evaluation Sample

| Sl no | Name of the students | University Roll No. | 1st Lecture | 2nd lecture | 3rd lecture | 4th lecture |
|---|---|---|---|---|---|---|
| 1 | X.Y | JISCE/2017/001 | 8.9 | 7.8 | 8.2 | 8.4 |
| 2 | | | | | | |

Weekly evaluation value = simple mean in scale of 10 = (8.9+7.8+8.2+8.4)/4 = 8.325

# FLIPPED LEARNING GUIDELINES

## PRE-CLASS

**Read and Complete the Activities**

- Read Learning Outcomes / Keywords
- Watch Video
- Read Article
- Do Prior-Knowledge Activity
- Do the Quiz

## IN-CLASS

**Participate, Question and Collaborate**

- Review the Video / Article
- Partcipate in the Activities
- Ask Questions
- Collaborate with Classmates

## POST-CLASS

**Put it into Practice**

- Devise Projects
- Create Portfolios
- Develop Presentations
- Compose Assignment
- Write Reflective Journals

# FLIPPED LEARNING GUIDELINES

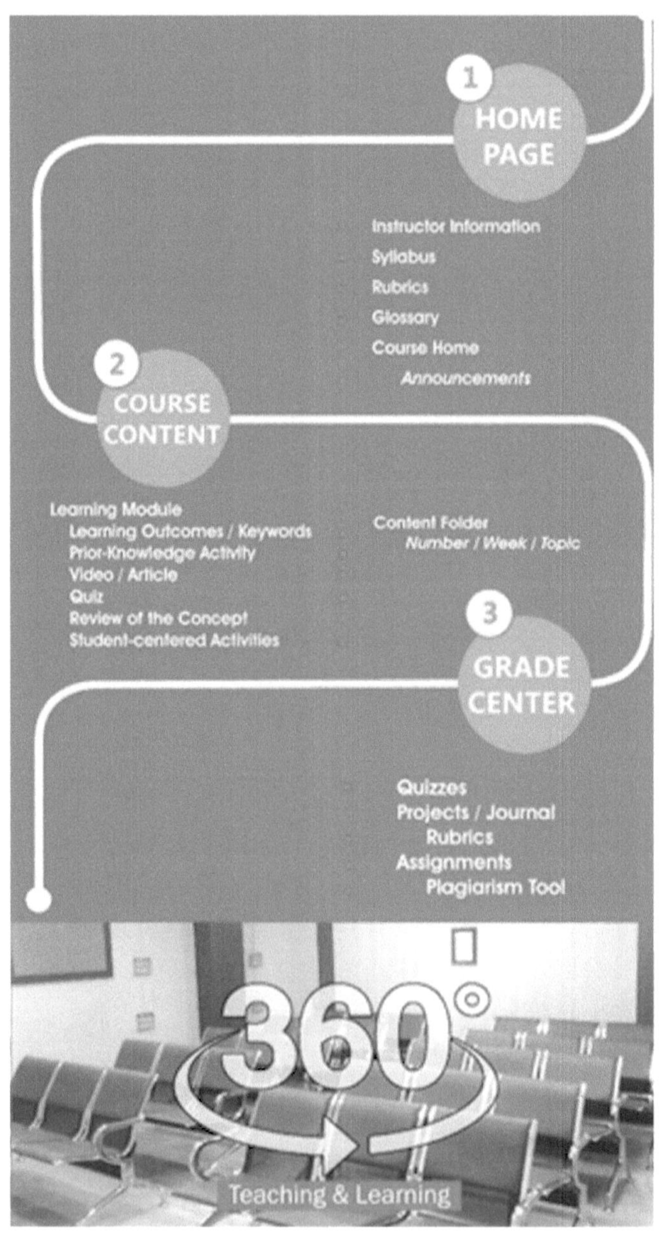

# APPENDIX-G

NEW YORK UNIVERSITY
https://www.nyu.edu/faculty/teaching-and-learning-resources/strategies-for-teaching-with-tech/flipped classes.html

**Steps to Flipping Your Class**

The goal of flipping your class is to practice a more student-centered pedagogy, thereby engaging your students in active learning experiences. In the flipped model, instructors structure 6 active learning environments that guide and support students as they work through them individually and collaborative. This is a process of reorganizing and redistributing content-related activities over sequences and cycles of in-class and out-of-class instructional practices and student experiences. In the context, appropriate uses of media and technology can play a valuable role.

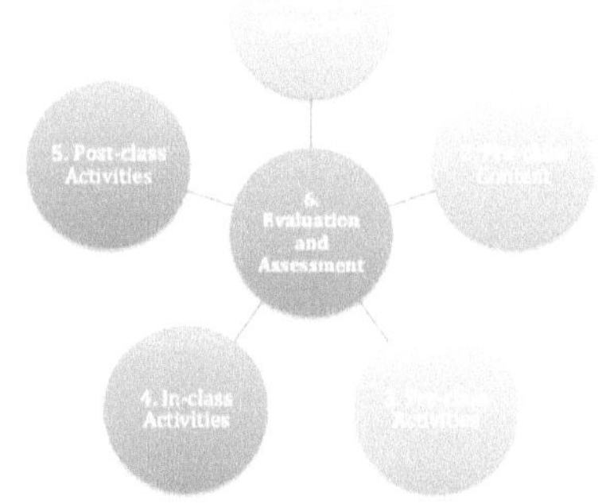


**Case Study of a Physics Lesson on Sound Intensity**

**PLAN & PREPARE LESSON**

**Step 1: Define Content Scope, Learning Objectives, & Instructional Strategies**

The success of your flipped class depends on the alignment of what you want your students to accomplish before, during, and after the class.

***What is the scope of your topic?*** Defining scope is important in terms of providing your students relevant and connected content that is not too granular or wide in terms of scope, otherwise students will have difficulty building a mental model and connecting content. Concept maps are useful exercises to help define scope. The biggest challenge is to determine how much of your subject matter can be taught within the time frame (e.g.; semester). Your goal should be to take the galaxy, so to speak, that makes up the breadth of your content and select the only most essential and relevant "constellations" of sub-topics that will make up a lesson. Each lesson should build or connect to the next within the sequence of the learning experience. For your flipped class you should select just one of these small "constellation" of sub-topics to focus the lesson. Think in terms of the amount of time needed to cover

NEW YORK UNIVERSITY

the material and time for the students to really learn it through application. Concept maps are useful exercises to help define scope as well as demarcate clusters of sub-topics that can be turned into digestible lessons.

***Defining Scope in Sound Example:*** A concept map was drawn to define the scope for the lesson on Sound Intensity. According to Mayer (2008), people learn more deeply when the information is broken into manageable and meaningful chunks. To create manageable and meaningful chunks for Sound Intensity it can be segmented into three goals; measurement of the intensity of a sound wave, measurement of intensity in relation to amplitude and distance, and measurement of intensity in decibels.

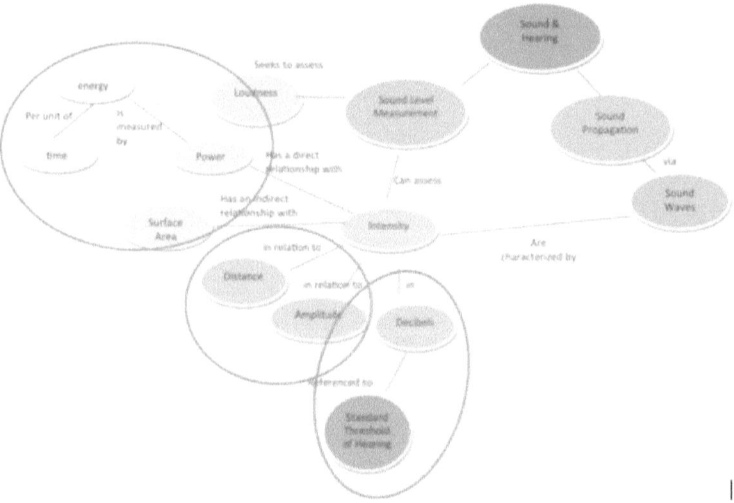


Scope of Lesson on Sound Intensity Using a Concept Map

***How will you contextualize the topic?*** Set expectations by preparing an explanation of how the new instructional material fits into the overall existing course structure. Students, especially adult learners, want to know why they are doing something, how it fits into the overall learning objectives, and used beyond the class. These explanations, of the process and how the new material fits into the course overall, provide vital contextual information to students.

***Contextualizing Sound Example***: Show students the concept map and how the lesson fits into the overall structure and sequence of the topic on Sound.

***How will students use or apply the material?*** Clearly write the learning objectives and outcomes that align with the activities students will do before, during, and after the class. It is not enough to for

students to just read, listen, watch, and take notes. They need to use it to really learn it. Consult *The Revised Bloom's Taxonomy* for selecting higher order action verbs to help write your learning objectives. What do you want your students to know and be able to do? And how will you assess what they know or can do?

*Learning Objectives Sequenced in Sound Example*:

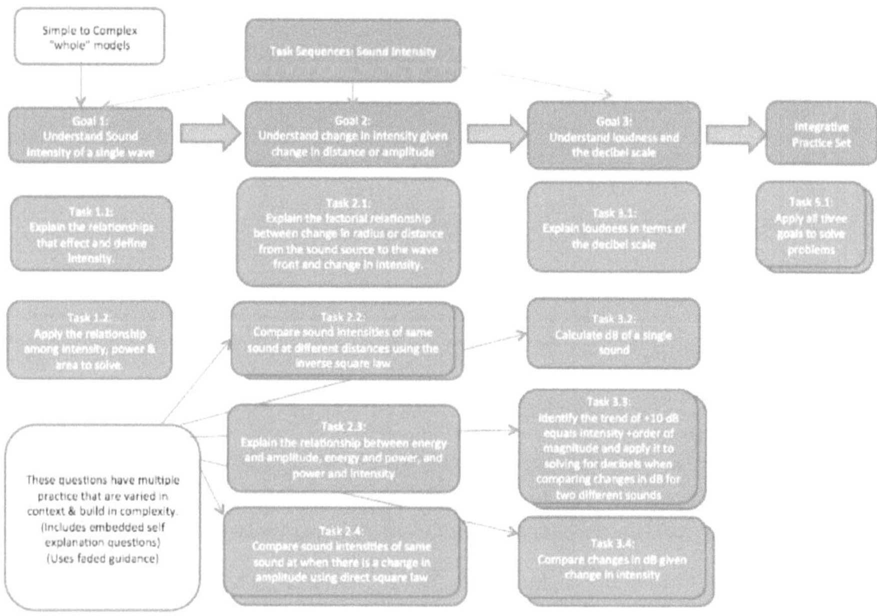


***How will students meet the learning objectives?*** Describe the task that matches the learning objective and goals.

***Aligning the Goals, Learning Objectives, and Tasks in Sound Intensity Example:***

***Learning Goal 1: Understand Sound Intensity of a Single Wave***

| ***Content Type*** | ***Learning Objective*** | ***Student Task*** | ***Instruction & Learning Format*** |
|---|---|---|---|
| ***Facts and Concepts:*** *The intensity of a sound wave is defined as the amount of power of that wave per unit surface area of the wave. I=P/A If the power remains constant why do sounds get softer the farther from the source? What is the relationship between intensity, power, energy, and amplitude at a fixed area?* ***Process/Concept Imagery:*** *What does it look like? How does it work?* ***Principle:*** *I = P/A and I = P/A* | *Students will explain the relationships that affect and define intensity....* | *...By manipulating the variables power and surface area in a simulation and observing the consequences in terms of intensity. [Task 1.1]* | *Direct instruction: Video/Animation explaining the concept + knowledge check questions.*<br><br>*Interactive instruction: Manipulative Simulation.* |
| ***Recurring and Non-recurring Procedures:*** $I = \frac{P\ (W)}{A\ (m)^2}$ $I = \frac{E/T}{4\pi r^2}$ | *Students will apply the relationships among intensity, power & area to solve...* | *...By analyze 4 different intensity relationships to find the one with the greatest or least magnitude. [Task 1.2] (Varied & Spaced Practice)* | *Direct Instruction: Worked Examples. Practice: Problem Solving Questions.* |

***Which instructional approach fits best for the main learning activity?*** Choose the evidence based instructional approach will fit the main learning activity (i.e.: peer-instruction, team-based learning, case-based learning, process-oriented guided inquiry learning)

***Instructional Approach for Sound Intensity Example:*** The main instructional approach for the Sound Intensity lesson will be **peer-to-peer instruction** while solving problems.

**Step 2: Student's gain familiarity with new material before class**

***What instructional materials and resources will you use for students to familiarize themselves with the content prior to class?*** Plan and prepare the new instructional materials that students will engage with prior to class. Ask yourself: What is the best way to communicate and present the new instructional material (e.g., video, text, animation, simulation, online multimedia module, or other). Will my students be able to process this content in this format effectively?

***Instructional Materials for Sound Intensity Example:*** Students will watch three animations on sound intensity. Each animation will target one of the three goals. Animations are chosen because of the complex conceptual nature of the content. It is difficult to convey these messages with just text and images. Additionally, worked examples will be provided for students to compare and contrast. Worked examples will be in text format because it will easier for students to process the entire example. Worked examples will be varied and increase in complexity.

**Step 3: Activities that motivate students to prepare before class**

***What kinds of activities will motivate students and prepare them for class?*** **Refer** to the learning objectives and tasks that you outlined in step 1. Ask yourself what incentives or motivation students will have to prepare for class and how you will know students have adequately prepared for the in-class activity.

***Pre-class activities for Sound Intensity Example:*** After viewing the animations, students will answer knowledge check questions after each animation. After studying worked examples students will explain the principles that arise from them. Students will identify an example that is incorrect and explain why it is incorrect. Students will also complete some partially worked examples that cover learning objectives in all three goals. Students will bring to class any questions they have about the concepts to help clarify them.

**Step 4: In-class activities that provide students opportunities to deepen understanding**

***What kind of in-class activities will focus students on attaining on higher-level cognitive abilities?*** Refer to the learning objectives and tasks that you outlined in step 1. Plan, prepare, and develop in-class activities that focus on higher-level cognitive activities. Will students be working individually in the classroom as you walk around and provide help or in groups to solve the problems or will you solve problems together as a group? The activity you choose will depend on the learning goals and objectives as some activities lend themselves best to certain types of content.

***In-class activities for Sound Intensity Example:*** At start of class instructor will elicit questions from

students based on pre-class activities and provide clarification. Next, students will independently solve full completion problems, post their answers online, and then converse with a peer on their problem-solving strategy. Problems will increase in complexity.

**Step 5: Post-class activities that extend student learning**

***How will students continue the learning experience from the inside class activity to outside of class?*** Refer to the learning objectives and tasks that you outlined in step 1. Plan, prepare and develop the continuation of the learning experience from the inside class activity to outside of class individual or collaborative practice. Determine what students should do after the in-class activity to continue learning or bridge to the next topic. We don't learn something very effectively in one instance. Rather we learn through practicing in a diversity of ways over an extended period of time. Think about and plan how often students will need to practice or revise their thinking to really master the material and be successful.

***Post-class activities that extend student learning for Sound Intensity Example:*** Students will continue to solve problems independently or with peers after class. These problems will be more complex.

**Step 6: Ongoing Evaluation and Assessment**

***How will you evaluate student's learning and progress?*** Evaluation and assessment are ongoing throughout the process. Plan how you will evaluate the effectiveness of the flipped experience and assess student understanding at all stages.

***Evaluation and Assessments for Sound Intensity Example:*** Instructor will review student work and assignment reports prior to class to anticipate any misconceptions or errors that will need to be addressed at start of class. Instructor will answer any questions students have during the main activity. Instructor will walk around the class as students solve problems independently or as they work in pairs in order to make him/herself available for guidance. Instructor will end the class with follow up instruction to any questions that were particularly difficult to answer and provide full expert explanations of problems. Instructor will post additional resources for students to use during the post-class activity and be available for office hours.

The instructor will evaluate him/herself in terms of the effectiveness to communicate complex concepts and explanations based on student results. Instructor will note any areas that still need to be communicated more clearly for future class sessions and iterations thereof.

**Ensure that all six of these steps are closely aligned and that they support the learning goals and objectives. Have a colleague or instructional designer review your plan and give you feedback.**

## Flipped Lesson Implementation Template

**Lesson Title:**

**Subject:**

**Level:**

**Prerequisite skills or knowledge** (connect to prior lesson):

**Time Requirements for First Exposure & Incentive:**
**Time Requirement for In-Class Activity:**
**Time Requirement for Post-Class Activity:**

**Technology & Materials for In-Class:** *Create a list of materials & room requirements you will need for the classroom such as clickers, internet access, computers, whiteboard, poster paper, etc.. Additionally consider if the room needs be arranged in a particular way for the activity to be successful. NYU Media Services can help you with many of these classroom technologies and room configurations.*

## Worksheet for preparing what an instructor will do before, during, and after the lesson

### 1. Implement pre-class materials

Using NYU Classes create a coherent online lesson for students to access in preparation for the in-class activity. Layout and sequence:

- Introduction to the topic
- Lesson map
- Lesson expectations & directions
- Learning objectives & outcomes
- New Instructional Material & Resources
- Incentive activity that prepares students for in-class activity

### 2. Review student work prior to class

Using NYU Classes review the student work prior to class. The pre-class incentive activities can provide the instructor with information about how to tailor the in-class activities to focus on the elements that students struggle with the most.

NEW YORK UNIVERSITY

For example: If you use the quiz tool in NYU Classes to engage students in problem solving activities, review the results prior to class to see where students may have difficulties or misconceptions. If you use the online discussion tool in NYU Classes to engage students in a pre-class discussion review the threads for depth of discussion and misconceptions.

**3. Establish your role before you head into the classroom**

Think about transitioning your role from leading the discussion or lecturer to letting your students take accountability for their learning and you become the guide, coach, and expert tutor. Here are some ways to become more of a guide:

- Walk around the classroom and observe the discussions
- Ask questions to confirm student understanding and draw out more discussion
- Answer questions that students bring to the class or raise during the class
- Moderate a debate or facilitate a group discussion
- Challenge students individually or challenge students to challenge each other

**4. Gather your materials for class**

Plan ahead for any technology you may need for the class. Use your checklist to gather all your materials. Be sure to contact Campus Media before the semester starts to get clickers, video conference requirements, or other special classroom needs.

**5. Start of class**

Take time at the beginning of the class to answer any questions student may have brought in preparation for class. Address areas students had the most trouble based on your review of their work.

**6. Implement the main in-class activity**

Implement your in-class activity plan by providing students clear directions and access to the materials they need to complete the in-class activity. Keep a close eye on the timeline you developed to keep students on task.

End the class by communicating the next steps students need to take after class.

**7. Implement post-class activity**

Use NYU Classes to implement the post-class activity. Layout and sequence:

- Directions for continuation of learning
- Extended learning activities that follow the in-class work

- Survey student motivation, confidence, and emotion

**8. Analyze the Data and Reflect on the Experience**

Evaluate the effectiveness of the model from various perspectives after implementation. In most cases, there will a product that is representative of students' work that can be used for evaluation. Connect the results of student assessment to the success of your lesson plan. There are three factors to consider during and after course delivery:

1) Effectiveness in terms of achieving the learning objectives
   - Have the learning outcomes been achieved?
   - What skills have been attained?
   - How effective was the delivery format (medium) in terms of communicating the message?
   - Were the instructors' presentations effective?
2) Relevance in terms of achieving satisfaction
   - Did the student's attitudes change between from the before, during, and after the course?
   - Could students connect the content to real contexts and use?
   - Were students impacted by the use of technology?
3) Efficiency in terms of the administrative part of the learning process?
   - Was the technology reliable?
   - Were the strategies optimal?
   - Was the scope and level of content appropriate and attainable for students?

Assess whether or not the learning objectives have been met. Connect the results of student assessment to the success of your lesson plan.

Keep a journal of what worked or did not work and how your would change the lesson the next time. Identify any areas in student learning that were still not as successful as you would have liked them to be and then brainstorm how to improve it. The results and quality of student will be in part a reflection on your teaching. Use that data to your advantage to make future changes and iterations. Teaching is a learning process that develops over time and with experience.

Involve others in your process for ideas and continued growth.

NEW YORK UNIVERSITY

## General Example Comparing Two Approaches

| | Instructor-Centered Approach | Student-Centered Approach (Flipped Class) |
|---|---|---|
| Before Class | Students work on homework connected to previous week's lecture. | Students are guided through new learning material that asks questions, provides immediate feedback, and collects questions in preparation for in-class activity. |
| | Instructor prepares new lecture. | Instructor reviews results of student work & prepares learning opportunities. |
| Start of Class | Students have limited knowledge about new lecture content or what to expect. | Students use their personally prepared questions to guide their own learning and take responsibility for it. |
| | Instructor has limited knowledge of student prior knowledge and thus makes assumptions about their needs. | Instructor uses student questions to address student specific needs. |
| During Class | Students listen, watch, take notes, and try to follow along. | Students practice applying the skills expected of them to learn. |
| | Instructor lectures new instructional material. | Instructor guides the educational process with feedback and provides short demonstrations or mini-lectures to clarify material when required. |
| After Class | Students work independently to assimilate lecture material (i.e.: homework), usually with delayed feedback. | Students continue applying knowledge and skills to more complex tasks. Students work individually or in small groups to solve problems or collaborate on projects. |
| | Instructor grades past homework. | Instructor posts any additional resources to help students. |
| Office Hours | Students grapple over what to study and request confirmation. | Students have the information about their learning progress and know where to seek help based on their analytics. |
| | Instructor repeats lecture content. | Instructor personalizes student learning by addressing a student's gap. |

NEW YORK UNIVERSITY

**List of Example Activities:** Note that these are just examples not tied to specific learning objectives. You would need to first identify specific learning objectives and then craft the online activities to align with those objectives.

| Techniques | Example of In-Class Activities | Example Online Activities | Collaborative or Interactive Tools for Online Activities |
|---|---|---|---|
| **One-alone** | | Student reads and annotates online journals | Link from NYU Classes to Library for students to access |
| | | Student analyzes & creates using online academic software | Google Docs, VCL |
| | | Student solves problems or answers questions | NYU Classes Question/Quiz/Survey Tool |
| | | Student watches, listens and takes notes of video (i.e.: lecture, interview, case-study) using online lessons or multimedia modules | NYU Classes Lesson tool; Commercial Software (Articulate Storyline; Adobe Captivate) |
| | | Student expresses ideas through blog or maintain an online journal | NYU Word Press; Google Sites. |
| | | Student interacts with a simulation to model prediction, statistics, and mathematics | Embed object in NYU Classes for students to access |
| | | Student interacts with data visualizations to analyze outcomes | Embed object in NYU Classes for students to access |
| **One-to-one** | Peer-to-peer teaching or sharing knowledge | Peer-to-peer teaching, review, or sharing knowledge | Google hangouts; Big Blue Button; NYU Classes Discussion tool; Google docs |
| | Students Interact with 2 player Games | Students Interact with 2 player Games | Embed & Access in NYU Classes |
| | | Student conducts and records interview of someone as part of an assignment | Student records using desktop screen share tools or video recorder; Posts on NYU Stream; Embeds in NYU Classes or submits as assignment |
| | Student works with a partner to collaborate on an assignment | Student works with a partner to collaborate on an assignment | Google hangouts; Big Blue Button; Google docs; VCL |

NEW YORK UNIVERSITY

| | | | |
|---|---|---|---|
| | Student role plays with another student | Student role plays with another student | Google hangouts; Big Blue Button; Record using NYU Stream; Embed in NYU Classes |
| | Student discusses ideas, solves problems, or answers questions with a partner [See Think, Pair, Share] | Student discusses ideas, solves problems, or answers questions with a partner. [See Think, Pair, Share] | Google hangouts; Big Blue Button; NYU Classes Discussion Tool |
| | Student solves problems independently during class while faculty walks around helping students individually. Can also be done during office hours or lab time. [See also Pro/Con Grid & use of Clickers in class] | Student solves problems independently during online office hours while faculty helps student. [See also Pro/Con Grid] | Google hangouts; Big Blue Button; NYU Classes Question/Quiz tool; NYU Classes Assignment Tool |
| | | Analyze video case-studies that demonstrate ethical issues and develop questions to share perspectives or develop an argument | Embed digital object in NYU Classes for students to access; Students post questions to partner using Discussion Tool in NYU Classes; |
| **One-to-many** | Symposium [Video Lecture capture for multi-location] | Student attends online symposium | Web Ex; Big Blue Button in NYU Classes |
| | Faculty member gives lecture to students; students listen and take notes during lecture | Student watch, listen and take notes on digital Lectures | Embed object in NYU Classes for students to access |
| | Student Role Play, Demonstration, or Presentation to class | Student Role Play, Demonstration, or Presentation to class | Students perform role plays using Google hangouts; Big Blue Button; Students record role play using NYU Stream and submit video through assignment in NYU Classes |
| | | Student conduct and record Interviews of a group of people. | Record using desktop screen share tools or video recorder; Post on NYU Stream; Embed in NYU Classes or submit as assignment |
| | | Student develops questions to share perspectives or develop an argument to share with class. | Google hangouts; Big Blue Button; NYU Classes Discussion tool; Google docs |
| **Many-to-many** | Students collaborate on assignments as a group [See send/pass a problem] | Students collaborate on assignments as a group | Google hangouts; Big Blue Button; Google docs; VCL |

NEW YORK UNIVERSITY

| | | | |
|---|---|---|---|
| | Students role play as a group | Students role play as a group | Google hangouts; Big Blue Button; Record using NYU Stream; Embed in NYU Classes |
| | Students partake in group discussions [Can also use Video conferencing for multi-location] | Students partake in group discussions | Google hangouts; Big Blue Button; NYU Classes Discussion Tool |
| | Students partake in group debates [Can also use Video conferencing for multi-location] | Students partake in group debates | Google hangouts; Big Blue Button; NYU Classes Discussion Tool |
| | Discuss Case Studies [text or video] | Watch & Discuss Case Studies (Video) | Embed & Access in NYU Classes; Discuss using: Google hangouts; Big Blue Button; NYU Classes Discussion Tool |
| | Students partake in group brainstorming sessions | Students partake in group brainstorming sessions | Google hangouts; Big Blue Button; NYU Classes Discussion tool; Google docs |

NEW YORK UNIVERSITY

**Thinking Skills for Use with Activities**

**Abstracting:** To find, identify, and explain general patterns in specific information or situations
- Identify what is important
- Summarize information wherever possible
- Find new information or situations where the general pattern applies

**Classifying/Categorizing:** Grouping items into categories on the basis of their attributes
- Identify items to classify
- State the rule for that category

**Constructing Support**: To provide support or proof of information
- Identify whether the information is fact or opinion
- Determine whether the situation needs support
- A supportive argument uses facts, evidence, examples, or appeals

**Analyzing Perspectives:** To describe reasons for your viewpoint or viewpoint of others
- On an issue of disagreement, first identify your own perspective
- Try to determine the reasons behind that perspective
- Identify a different perspective
- Try to determine the reasons or logic behind that perspective

**Deductive Reasoning:** Identify specific examples to support a general statement, rule, or principle
- Identify the generalizations or predictions that apply to the situation
- Identify the conditions, reasons or proof that have to be in place for that generalization to occur
- If the information is true and the reasoning valid, the conclusions must be true

**Inductive Reasoning:** Inferring unknown generalizations from information or observations
- Make a general statement that explains observed patterns

**Error Analysis:** To find and describe errors in your own thinking/performance or the thinking/performance of others
- Determine if the information is trying to persuade, change behavior, or is based on facts
- Look for errors in the claims or steps of the process. If errors are found explain how to fix them.

**Comparing/Contrasting:** Identifying and explaining similarities and differences among items
- Explain how items are similar and different with respect to characteristics
- Summarize what has been learned

# APPENDIX-H

EDUCAUSE LEARNING INITIATIVE

## 7 THINGS YOU SHOULD KNOW ABOUT...™ FLIPPED CLASSROOMS

### Scenario

For the past two weeks, Kyle has been taking a flipped course in designing food gardens. Before he attends each class, he watches videos of short lectures recorded or recommended by his instructor. Each lecture comes with a brief online quiz that offers him immediate feedback on whether he missed any essential points. Today as he enters class, he glances at the schedule on the whiteboard. For the first half hour, teams will discuss how the content of the video lectures on microclimates, insect predation, and disease control will inform their team projects. Professor Dalton circulates among the tables to see if anyone has questions.

Kyle's team will be repurposing an area the size of an urban backyard into a visually appealing garden that is also a functional food source. It's part of the larger class project to reclaim a strip of city land by building a demonstration food garden. "I think we should bring in disease-resistant blueberries, grapes, and pome fruits," says Coleen, looking at the rough drawings they have made so far. Dalton stops to look over their design. "Check the nursery catalogs on the front table," he suggests. "Disease-resistant strains are clearly marked in their listings." As they search the catalog and discuss which diseases might be a problem in dwarf apples, pears, blueberries, and grapes, Kyle enters their cultivar choices in their Google Docs space. They are turning to a discussion of microclimates and plant placement when a chime signals discussion is over.

In the second half of the class, team monitors each retrieve two flat boxes from the front of the class. One box contains a stack of pins and various leaves preserved in plastic. The second box has a foam insert topped by a paper grid; each square is labeled with a nutritional deficiency or a disease common to food plants. During the next half hour, each team is to identify the disease or nutritional deficiency and pin the correct leaf in the right spot on the grid. Dalton is on hand, directing attention to clues and sometimes challenging their choices.

As he leaves, Kyle reflects that the hands-on activities have given him a far better grasp of the information and more confidence in what he has learned than he could have gotten from an in-class lecture.

### 1 What is it?

**The flipped classroom is a pedagogical model in which the typical lecture and homework elements of a course are reversed.** Short video lectures are viewed by students at home before the class session, while in-class time is devoted to exercises, projects, or discussions. The video lecture is often seen as the key ingredient in the flipped approach, such lectures being either created by the instructor and posted online or selected from an online repository. While a prerecorded lecture could certainly be a podcast or other audio format, the ease with which video can be accessed and viewed today has made it so ubiquitous that the flipped model has come to be identified with it.

The notion of a flipped classroom draws on such concepts as active learning, student engagement, hybrid course design, and course podcasting. The value of a flipped class is in the repurposing of class time into a workshop where students can inquire about lecture content, test their skills in applying knowledge, and interact with one another in hands-on activities. During class sessions, instructors function as coaches or advisors, encouraging students in individual inquiry and collaborative effort.

### 2 How does it work?

There is no single model for the flipped classroom—**the term is widely used to describe almost any class structure that provides prerecorded lectures followed by in-class exercises**. In one common model, students might view multiple lectures of five to seven minutes each. Online quizzes or activities can be interspersed to test what students have learned. Immediate quiz feedback and the ability to rerun lecture segments may help clarify points of confusion. Instructors might lead in-class discussions or turn the classroom into a studio where students create, collaborate, and put into practice what they learned from the lectures they view outside class. As on-site experts, instructors suggest various approaches, clarify content, and monitor progress. They might organize students into an ad hoc workgroup to solve a problem that several are struggling to understand. Because this approach represents a comprehensive change in the class dynamic, some instructors have chosen to implement only a few elements of the flipped model or to flip only a few selected class sessions during a term.

### 3 Who's doing it?

**A growing number of higher education individual faculty have begun using the flipped model in their courses.** At Algonquin College, a video production class has been using this model to explain the workings of editing software, a procedure that is notoriously difficult to explain in a standard lecture. Short tutorial video lectures let students move at their own pace, rewind to review portions, and skip through sections they already understand,

more >>



educause.edu/eli

meaning students come to class able to use the software and prepared to do creative projects with their peers. A particularly successful example of a blended and flipped class in accounting at Penn State accommodates 1,300 students. In-class time is used for open discussion, a featured guest speaker, or hands-on problem solving where instructor support is supplemented by student assistants. At Harvard University, one physics professor not only employs the flipped model but has also developed a correlative site, Learning Catalytics, that provides instructors with free interactive software enabling students to discuss, apply, and get feedback from what they hear in lecture.

## 4 Why is it significant?

In a traditional lecture, students often try to capture what is being said at the instant the speaker says it. They cannot stop to reflect upon what is being said, and they may miss significant points because they are trying to transcribe the instructor's words. By contrast, the use of video and other prerecorded media puts lectures under the control of the students: they can watch, rewind, and fast-forward as needed. This ability may be of particular value to students with accessibility concerns, especially where captions are provided for those with hearing impairments. Lectures that can be viewed more than once may also help those for whom English is not their first language. **Devoting class time to application of concepts might give instructors a better opportunity to detect errors in thinking**, particularly those that are widespread in a class. At the same time, collaborative projects can encourage social interaction among students, making it easier for them to learn from one another and for those of varying skill levels to support their peers.

## 5 What are the downsides?

The flipped classroom is an easy model to get wrong. Although the idea is straightforward, **an effective flip requires careful preparation**. Recording lectures requires effort and time on the part of faculty, and out-of-class and in-class elements must be carefully integrated for students to understand the model and be motivated to prepare for class. As a result, introducing a flip can mean additional work and may require new skills for the instructor, although this learning curve could be mitigated by entering the model slowly.

Students, for their part, have been known to complain about the loss of face-to-face lectures, particularly if they feel the assigned video lectures are available to anyone online. Students with this perspective may not immediately appreciate the value of the hands-on portion of the model, wondering what their tuition brings them that they could not have gotten by surfing the web. Those who see themselves as attending class to hear lectures may feel it is safe to skip a class that focuses on activities and might miss the real value of the flip. Finally, even where students embrace the model, their equipment and access might not always support rapid delivery of video.

## 6 Where is it going?

As the flipped class becomes more popular, **new tools may emerge to support the out-of-class portion of the curriculum**. In particular, the ongoing development of powerful mobile devices will put a wider range of rich, educational resources into the hands of students, at times and places that are most convenient for them. Greater numbers of courses will likely employ elements of the flipped classroom, supplementing traditional out-of-class work with video presentations and supporting project-based and lab-style efforts during regular class times. At a certain level of adoption, colleges and universities may need to take a hard look at class spaces to ensure they support the kinds of active and collaborative work common in flipped classes.

## 7 What are the implications for teaching and learning?

The flipped classroom constitutes a role change for instructors, who give up their front-of-the-class position in favor of a more collaborative and cooperative contribution to the teaching process. There is a concomitant change in the role of students, many of whom are used to being cast as passive participants in the education process, where instruction is served to them. **The flipped model puts more of the responsibility for learning on the shoulders of students while giving them greater impetus to experiment.** Activities can be student-led, and communication among students can become the determining dynamic of a session devoted to learning through hands-on work. What the flip does particularly well is to bring about a distinctive shift in priorities—from merely covering material to working toward mastery of it.

EDUCAUSE®

EDUCAUSE 7 Things You Should Know About...™

EDUCAUSE is a nonprofit membership association created to support those who lead, manage, and use information technology to benefit higher education. A comprehensive range of resources and activities are available to all EDUCAUSE members. For more information about EDUCAUSE, including membership, please contact us at info@educause.edu or visit educause.edu.

# BIOGRAPHY

| | |
|---|---|
| **NAME** | Namita Sravat |
| | ACADEMIC **BACKGROUND**<br>Master of Science,<br>Asian Institute of Technology, Thailand (1997).<br>Bachelor of Architecture,<br>Amravati University, India (1991) |
| **EXPERIENCES** | Academic Administration, Academic Curriculum Review and Development, Academic Regulations and Procedures, Faculty Evaluation Processes and Procedures, Academic Institute's Board of Trustees Related Matters. |

www.ingramcontent.com/pod-product-compliance
Ingram Content Group UK Ltd.
Pitfield, Milton Keynes, MK11 3LW, UK
UKHW041855190726
13854UKWH00002B/924